Relatively Close

by James Sherman

A Samuel French Acting Edition

SAMUEL FRENCH

FOUNDED 1830

NEW YORK HOLLYWOOD LONDON TORONTO

SAMUELFRENCH.COM

Copyright © 2011 by James Sherman
ALL RIGHTS RESERVED

CAUTION: Professionals and amateurs are hereby warned that *RELATIVELY CLOSE* is subject to a licensing fee. It is fully protected under the copyright laws of the United States of America, the British Commonwealth, including Canada, and all other countries of the Copyright Union. All rights, including professional, amateur, motion picture, recitation, lecturing, public reading, radio broadcasting, television and the rights of translation into foreign languages are strictly reserved. In its present form the play is dedicated to the reading public only.

The amateur and professional live stage performance rights to *RELATIVELY CLOSE* are controlled exclusively by Samuel French, Inc., and licensing arrangements and performance licenses must be secured well in advance of presentation. PLEASE NOTE that amateur licensing fees are set upon application in accordance with your producing circumstances. When applying for a licensing quotation and a performance license please give us the number of performances intended, dates of production, your seating capacity and admission fee. Licensing fees are payable one week before the opening performance of the play to Samuel French, Inc., at 45 W. 25th Street, New York, NY 10010.

Licensing fee of the required amount must be paid whether the play is presented for charity or gain and whether or not admission is charged.

Professional/Stock licensing fees quoted upon application to Samuel French, Inc.

For all other rights than those stipulated above, apply to: Harden-Curtis Associates, 850 Seventh Avenue, Suite 903, New York, NY 10019 Attn: Mary Harden.

Particular emphasis is laid on the question of amateur or professional readings, permission and terms for which must be secured in writing from Samuel French, Inc.

Copying from this book in whole or in part is strictly forbidden by law, and the right of performance is not transferable.

Whenever the play is produced the following notice must appear on all programs, printing and advertising for the play: "Produced by special arrangement with Samuel French, Inc."

Due authorship credit must be given on all programs, printing and advertising for the play.

ISBN 978-0-573-69955-9   Printed in U.S.A.   #29860

No one shall commit or authorize any act or omission by which the copyright of, or the right to copyright, this play may be impaired.

No one shall make any changes in this play for the purpose of production.

Publication of this play does not imply availability for performance. Both amateurs and professionals considering a production are strongly advised in their own interests to apply to Samuel French, Inc., for written permission before starting rehearsals, advertising, or booking a theatre.

No part of this book may be reproduced, stored in a retrieval system, or transmitted in any form, by any means, now known or yet to be invented, including mechanical, electronic, photocopying, recording, videotaping, or otherwise, without the prior written permission of the publisher.

MUSIC USE NOTE

Licensees are solely responsible for obtaining formal written permission from copyright owners to use copyrighted music in the performance of this play and are strongly cautioned to do so. If no such permission is obtained by the licensee, then the licensee must use only original music that the licensee owns and controls. Licensees are solely responsible and liable for all music clearances and shall indemnify the copyright owners of the play and their licensing agent, Samuel French, Inc., against any costs, expenses, losses and liabilities arising from the use of music by licensees.

IMPORTANT BILLING AND CREDIT REQUIREMENTS

All producers of *RELATIVELY CLOSE* must give credit to the Author of the Play in all programs distributed in connection with performances of the Play, and in all instances in which the title of the Play appears for the purposes of advertising, publicizing or otherwise exploiting the Play and/or a production. The name of the Author *must* appear on a separate line on which no other name appears, immediately following the title and *must* appear in size of type not less than fifty percent of the size of the title type.

In addition, the following credits must appear in all programs distributed in connection with the work:

Relatively Close was originally produced by Victory Gardens Theater, Chicago, IL. Dennis Začek, Artistic Director.

RELATIVELY CLOSE received its co-world premiere at the Center for Performing Arts at Illinois State University in Normal, IL. on November 11, 2007. The Director was Don LaCasse. The set design was by John C. Stark. The lighting design was by Sarah Hamilton. The costume design was by Caitie Entwsitle. The acting coach was Janet Wilson. The sound design was by Valerie Lawrence. The production stage manager was Susana Pelayo. The cast was as follows:

RON	Nick Demeris
MARLENE	Anne Thompson
JAN	Katy Morehouse
YOUSEF	Gabriel Swee
BETH	Amanda Roeder
ARTHUR	Carthy Dixon
DYLAN	Dave Gonzalez

RELATIVELY CLOSE received its co-world premiere at the Victory Gardens Theater in Chicago, IL. on June 16, 2008. The director was Dennis Zacek. The set design was by John C. Stark. The lighting design was by Julie Mack. The costume design was by Christine Pascual. The sound design was by Andre Pluess. the production stage manager was Tina M. Jach. The cast was as follows:

RON	Daniel Cantor
MARLENE	Wendi Weber
JAN	Penny Slusher
YOUSEF	Usman Ally
BETH	Laura T. Fisher
ARTHUR	Dexter Zollicoffer
DYLAN	Dave Gonzalez

CHARACTERS

JAN - The eldest sister, 47 years old
BETH - The middle sister, 45 years old
MARLENE - The youngest sister, 44 years old
YOUSEF - Jan's husband, Iranian-American
ARTHUR - Beth's husband, African-American
RON - Marlene's husband, Jewish-American
DYLAN - Beth's son from a previous marriage, 15

SETTING

A two-story home in Union Pier, Michigan.

TIME

This summer.

PUNCTUATION POINTS

A period is a period. An ellipsis (...) means that the speaker stops speaking of his/her own accord. A dash (-) means the the speaker is interrupted by the next speaker. A slash (/) in a line means that the next speaker starts speaking while the current speaker is still speaking. Dialogue in two columns means that two speakers are speaking at the same time.

ACT 1

Scene 1

(At rise: The house is dark. After a moment, the front door opens and **MARLENE** *enters, being hustled in by* **RON**.*)*

RON. *(offstage)* Forget the luggage. Go on. Go on. Get in there.

MARLENE. I'm in. I'm in.

RON. All right.

(He stops her and himself.)

(calling out to the house) Hello?

(No response.)

Yesss.

(to **MARLENE***)* Okay. You're here first. You choose.

(The sound of a toilet flush is heard.)

JAN. *(offstage)* Hello-o?

RON. *(pissed off)* Goddamit.

(From an upstairs bedroom, **JAN** *enters.)*

JAN. *(calling)* Hello!
RON. *(cheerfully)* Hi!
MARLENE. Hi.
JAN. Hi!

*(***JAN** *comes downstairs.)*

RON. Shit.

*(***JAN** *enters and goes to* **MARLENE**.*)*

JAN. Hi.

MARLENE. Hi.

(They hug.)

JAN. *(to* **RON***)* Hey, Ron.

RON. Hi. Nice to see you.

(They hug.)

JAN. I took Mom and Dad's room. You don't mind, do you?

MARLENE.	**RON.**
No.	Nooooo!

MARLENE. You got here first. You get to choose.

JAN. I mean, no point in it sitting empty, right? We figured someone should take it.

RON. Yeah, so did we.

JAN. "First come, first served." *(rhetorically)* Whad'ya gonna do?

RON. I didn't see your car.

JAN. Oh, Joe took it to get washed already.

(quoting **JOE***)* "We drove through Gary. The car is dirty."

(as herself) Joe and his cars.

(rhetorically) Whad'ya gonna do?

Well, you guys look good.

MARLENE. So do you.

JAN. Oh, god, no. I've been eating so much chazerai. "On the campaign trail."

(rhetorically) Whad'ya gonna do?

RON. I'm going to get our stuff.

*(***RON** *exits.)*

JAN. *(to* **MARLENE***)* So...Here we are again.

MARLENE. Yeah. It's strange to be here without Dad.

JAN. *(shrugs)* Yeah. Well, really, after Mom died, it was strange to be here with Dad, wasn't it?

(looking around) What are we going to do with this place?

MARLENE. We have all week to talk about it.

JAN. What's there to talk about?

MARLENE. How're the boys?

JAN. The boys? Ohmigod. Well, you know Cyrus is working with Joe. He's doing great. Everybody in the office thinks he's a genius.

*(**RON** enters with luggage.)*

And Sammy is at overnight camp. He's having the time of his life.

RON. Sammy's at camp? What's he doing, like, making you a lanyard?

JAN. A what?

RON. That's what I did in camp. Arts and crafts. Boating. Archery.

JAN. Archery? Oh, God, no. Sammy's at Financial Camp. They teach him how to play the stock market, they take field trips to the Board of Trade, and at the end of six weeks, each kid has his own portfolio.

RON. *(to **MARLENE**, sardonically)* And you worry about the next generation.

JAN. *(back to business)* So. Which room do you want?

MARLENE. Um...

*(She looks to **RON**.)*

RON. Whatever.

MARLENE. The Gold Room?

RON. Whatever.

JAN. Why don't you take the Green Room? Then Beth can take the Gold Room.

MARLENE. There're twin beds in the Gold Room.

JAN. Exactly. Let her and the new husband sleep in twin beds. I don't need to listen to them going at it all night long. Remember when she was here with Mike, the Musician?

(imitating) "OH! OH! OH!"

JAN. *(herself)* All night long. I couldn't believe it. I didn't sleep a wink. Remember?

MARLENE. No.

JAN. Oh, are you kidding? You must.

> *(to* **RON***)*
>
> You remember that, don't you?

RON. Yes.

MARLENE. Well, she's not going to want to sleep in the Gold Room. Maybe Dylan'll take the Gold Room.

JAN. What? She's bringing Dylan?

MARLENE. Didn't you know that?

JAN. She's bringing Dylan? Ohmigod. That kid gives me the creeps. Why is she bringing Dylan?

MARLENE. She wants him and Arthur to have time together.

JAN. Well...maybe he'll like this husband better than the last one.

MARLENE. Or the one before that.

JAN. Or the one before that.

MARLENE. Or the one before that.

JAN. & MARLENE. *(in unison, mock-screaming like they're in a monster movie)* AHHHHHHHHHHH!

> *(They enjoy the moment.* **RON** *heads upstairs with the luggage and* **JAN** *and* **MARLENE** *follow.)*

JAN. Have you met him yet?

MARLENE. Arthur? No. Ron has.

RON. Yeah.

JAN. You've met him?

RON. I was at the wedding.

JAN. You were at the wedding?

RON. I was at the wedding.

JAN. What do you think?

RON. Oh, he's a great guy. Brilliant scholar. They seem very much in love. I give it six months.

JAN. *(trying to remember)* What does he do?

RON. He's a provost.

JAN. What is that?

RON. I have no idea. He works for a university. Some kind of administrative thing.

JAN. And what does he do?

RON. I don't know. Whatever a provost does.

JAN. Which is what?

RON. I don't know!

JAN. All right. All right.

MARLENE. Well, better to be a pro-vost, than an anti-vost.

(**MARLENE** *laughs. The others do not.*)

JAN. Yeah, whatever. Well...I'll let you get settled in. I'm still unpacking myself. I started a grocery list. Add whatever you want to the list.

RON. I just like to have some Diet Coke.

JAN. Well, put down whatever you want. When Joe gets back, we'll go shopping.

(**JAN** *goes to her room.*)

(**RON** *looks to* **MARLENE**.)

RON. Can we go now?

MARLENE. It'll be all right.

RON. I've been here five minutes, I'm already pissed off.

(*mocking* **JAN**)

"First come, first served. Whad'ya gonna do?"

(*himself*)

I'll tell you what I'm gonna do.

MARLENE. Be nice.

RON. What did we say? We said we'd all get here at noon. I got here at noon. I bet they got here at five o'clock this morning just so they could get your parents' bedroom. It's not fair.

(**MARLENE** *goes to him.*)

MARLENE. Hey. This is time for us.

RON. Time for us? With all those other people hanging around?

MARLENE. Would you like it if it was just us?

RON. Sure. We'd get your parents' bedroom.

(He goes back to unpacking. The sound of a car approaching. **MARLENE** *looks out the window.)*

MARLENE. Here comes Joe.

RON. What's he driving?

*(***RON** *looks out the window.)*

That is big.

(The sound of a car stopping and the door opening and closing.)

RON. Oh, shit.

MARLENE. What?

*(***RON** *goes to the door.)*

RON. They brought the dog.

*(***RON** *exits, runs downstairs, goes to the door, and calls out.)*

You can't bring the dog in here.

YOUSEF. *(offstage)* I know. I just want to–

RON. No. Seriously.

YOUSEF. *(offstage)* I just–

RON. Please. Can you just take her in the back?

YOUSEF. *(offstage)* I'm going to take her in the back. I just–

RON. Well, can you take her around that way?

YOUSEF. *(offstage)* Can't I just–

RON. No. Please.

YOUSEF. *(offstage)* All right. All right.

(to the dog)

Come on, Fifi!

*(***RON** *goes to the back porch to see that* **YOUSEF** *has arrived in the back of the house.)*

RON. Is there some place you can...?

YOUSEF. *(offstage)* Yes. Yes. She'll stay out here.

RON. You've got to keep her out there.

YOUSEF. *(offstage)* I know. I'm tying her up.

(to the dog)

Come here! Come here, Fifi... Stay!... Stay there!... Stay!

(YOUSEF enters.)

YOUSEF. Hello. How are you?

(YOUSEF and RON shake hands.)

RON. I'm fine. How're you doing?

YOUSEF. I'm fine.

RON. I just can't have the dog in the house.

YOUSEF. I know.

RON. 'Cause I'm allergic.

YOUSEF. I know.

RON. You bring the dog in, I'm going to clog right up.

YOUSEF. You don't have pills?

(RON goes to close the front door.)

RON. No, I can take medication for it. But it counteracts with my anti-depressants. I'm a wreck. You don't want to see it. *(referring out)* That's a nice looking car.

YOUSEF. It's an Escalade. It's made by Cadillac.

(JAN has come out of her room and comes downstairs.)

JAN. *(to YOUSEF)* Where'd you get lost?

YOUSEF. I didn't get lost.

(referring to RON and himself)

We're talking.

(to RON)

It's a 6.2 liter -

YOUSEF.
V8 engine. I got room for six, seven, even eight people at one time. And the seats are all brushed leather. The finest leather in any car. It's like sitting on a sofa while you're driving. It's like driving a sofa.

JAN.
(to RON)
Joe and his cars. Whad'ya gonna do? The day the car comes out, he's got to get it. Like the first kid on the block with the new toy. He's got to be the first one with the new toy. He's just a big kid at heart.

(**MARLENE** *has come downstairs.*)

MARLENE. Hi, Yousef.

YOUSEF. Hello. How are you?

(They hug.)

RON. He was just telling me about his new car.

YOUSEF. *(to MARLENE)* It's an Escalade.

JAN. She doesn't care.

MARLENE. No, I...

JAN. You don't care. It's a car.

MARLENE. How are things going with the new house?

YOUSEF.
Oh! Those sons of bitches. I'm going to kill those guys. They say they're going to show up. They don't show up. And then they show up and work for two days and then for two weeks they don't show up.

JAN.
Oh! I can't wait for you to see it. I'm finally going to have my house. How many buildings has he built in the last fifteen years. I've been waiting my turn. I'm like the cobbler's children. Whad'ya gonna do?

JAN. *(to YOUSEF)* What are you complaining about?

YOUSEF. I'm not complaining.

RON. Well, we can't wait to see it.

JAN. *(to YOUSEF)* Come help me unpack.

(to RON and MARLENE)

Go write down what you want from the store.

(MARLENE and RON go to the kitchen. JAN and YOUSEF go upstairs.)

(to YOUSEF) I told them when Beth and Arthur get here, once they write down what they want from the store, we'll go get it.

YOUSEF. Why did you tell them that?

JAN. Get up here.

(JAN and YOUSEF go into their bedroom. MARLENE and RON are in the kitchen.)

MARLENE. What should I put down?

RON. Just put down Diet Coke for me. You put down whatever you want.

(MARLENE thinks and writes. Upstairs in their bedroom, are JAN and YOUSEF.)

YOUSEF. Can we go now?

JAN. What's your problem?

YOUSEF. These people in your family. They're crazy.

JAN. It's only for a week. You can stand them for a week. And be nice.

YOUSEF. I'm nice.

JAN. I've got to get Beth and Marlene to agree with me.

YOUSEF. *(ironically)* Yes. Let me know when that happens.

(JAN gives YOUSEF a snide look.)

MARLENE. *(to RON)* Anything else you want?

RON. Yeah. I want an -- *(mimicking YOUSEF's accent)* Escalade-uh.

MARLENE. Be nice.

RON. It kills me when he says, "Escalade-uh." It's Escalade. He says, "Escalade-uh." I think he's talking about a moving staircase.

MARLENE. It's his accent.

RON. It's not his accent. It's because he's so rich, he can afford extra syllables.

(A car horn is heard.)

MARLENE. That must be Beth.

RON. *(to MARLENE)* Great. Your other crazy sister.

> (**MARLENE** *puts down her pen, goes upstairs and goes into her room. The front door opens.* **BETH** *and* **ARTHUR** *enter.*)

BETH. Anybody home?

RON. *(cheerfully)* Hi!

> (**RON** *goes to greet* **BETH**. **BETH** *shakes hands with* **RON**.)

BETH. Ron. Hi.

RON. Hi. How're you doing?

BETH. Nice to see you.

> (**ARTHUR** *comes up behind* **BETH**.)

BETH. *(continuing)* You remember Arthur.

RON. Of course.

> (**RON** *and* **ARTHUR** *shake hands.*)

RON. *(continuing)* Nice to see you.

ARTHUR. Pleasure to see you again.

> (**JAN** *and* **YOUSEF** *enter.*)

JAN. Here are the lovebirds.

> (*She goes to* **BETH** *and they hug.*)

BETH. Hi.

JAN. Hi. Oh, you look wonderful.

BETH. So do you.

JAN. Oh, please.

BETH. *(to YOUSEF)* Hi, Joe.

YOUSEF. Hello. How are you?

BETH. Jan. Joe. I'd like you to meet Arthur.

> (**ARTHUR** *shakes hands with* **JAN**.)

ARTHUR. How / do you do?

JAN. Hi, I'm Jan Levy, candidate for alderman of the 43rd ward. Hope I can count on your vote.

ARTHUR. We don't live in your ward.

JAN. Hey, it's Chicago. We can work around that.

ARTHUR. Umm...Okay.

    (**ARTHUR** *and* **YOUSEF** *shake hands.*)

YOUSEF. Hello. How are you?

ARTHUR. How do you do?

JAN. You got here okay?

BETH. Fine. No problem. We'd like to get settled in.

JAN. Of course. Come in. Get settled in.

BETH. Can we have Mom and Dad's room?

JAN. Oh, you know what? Joe and I are already in there. "First come, first served."

BETH.	**JAN.**
"First come, first served?"	Whad'ya gonna do?

BETH. That's not a rule.

JAN. That's always the rule.

BETH. When we were kids.

JAN. I'm young at heart.

BETH. Well, if I would've known that, we would've come here earlier.

RON. Wouldn't have mattered.

BETH. *(to* **JAN***)* Could we please–

JAN. We're already unpacked.

BETH. I'll help you move.

JAN. Oh, I don't want you to bother.

BETH. This is Arthur's first time here. I thought it'd be nice if–

JAN. We're already in there. Leeny and Ron are in the Green Room. You and Arthur can have the Gold Room.

BETH. The Gold Room? The Gold Room? All right, look... You didn't give us a wedding present. Let this be / your wedding present to us.

JAN. I didn't give you a – ? We most certainly did send you a wedding present.

BETH. No. You didn't.

JAN. I know we sent you something.

BETH. No.

JAN. *(to YOUSEF)* I'm telling you. That Barbara of yours. She's out to get me. You've got to fire her.

YOUSEF. I'm going to do that.

JAN. *(to BETH)* So I made a list who cooks dinner each night. I'm going to do tonight, okay? And I started a grocery list. You write down anything you want and we'll go get it. Anything you want.

BETH. *(to ARTHUR)* Do you want anything?

ARTHUR. Occasionally, I like to have a Diet Coke.

(RON raises his hand.)

RON. My man!

(RON holds his hand up to do a high-five. ARTHUR doesn't respond. RON lowers his hand.)

BETH. *(to JAN)* Maybe we'll do our own dinners.

JAN. No. No. I want to do it. So, come on. You two should get settled in.

RON. Beth. I thought you were bringing Dylan.

BETH. Yes. We did.

(She looks around.)

Where is he?

ARTHUR. He's still outside.

BETH. He's – ?

(She turns and peers outside.)

BETH. *(continuing; calling out)* Oh, Honey. Come on in.

(DYLAN enters.)

JAN. *(to DYLAN)* Well...What a nice surprise to have you here with us.

BETH. *(to DYLAN)* Honey, you remember your Auntie Jan and Uncle Yousef.

YOUSEF. *(to DYLAN)* Hello. How are you?

(He holds out his hand to shake hands with **DYLAN**. **DYLAN** *gives him a quick one.)*

DYLAN. Hey.

BETH. *(to* **DYLAN***)* And your Uncle Ron.

*(***DYLAN** *and* **RON** *shake hands.)*

RON. Hey.

DYLAN. Hey.

RON. I like the bling.

BETH. Dylan's been writing poetry. He was in a Poetry Slam in school.

(to **DYLAN***)*

Honey, maybe you'll do some of your poetry for us.

ARTHUR. Oh, that would be great. Dylan...I wager you'll get a lot of writing done this week. In this beautiful setting. Connected to nature. Puts me in mind of "*Walden Pond.*"

(quoting) "I came to the woods because I wanted to live my life deliberately."

DYLAN. Where's a TV?

BETH. In the basement.

ARTHUR. *(to* **DYLAN***)* Dylan, would you like to help me with the luggage?

DYLAN. No.

ARTHUR. Okay.

DYLAN. Where's the basement?

JAN. We'll show you. We were going down there anyway. Joe, show him where the light is.

*(***DYLAN** *and* **YOUSEF** *exit to the basement.)*

(to **BETH***)* You know, while we're here this week, I thought we'd empty out the basement. Get rid of all those boxes and stuff.

BETH. You mean Mom and Dad's stuff?

JAN. Well, sure. It's all junk now anyway, right? I'm just going to go–

(*JAN exits to the basement.*)

RON. So...

BETH. Where's Marlene?

RON. She's upstairs. There's a new person here, so...

ARTHUR. Oh, yes. Beth told me Marlene is very shy.

RON. Well, it's way past shy. She has SAD.

ARTHUR. Oh. Well, perhaps I can cheer her up.

RON. No, no. She's not sad. She has SAD. Social Affective Disorder. You're a new person, so she has to meet you in her own way.

BETH. Wait, wait. She brought the thing?

RON. Of course.

BETH. Oh, for...

(*BETH goes upstairs. RON and ARTHUR are alone.*)

RON. She just needs a little encouragement. After she gets past the first encounter with you, she'll be fine.

ARTHUR. Fascinating.

(*BETH knocks on MARLENE's door and enters.*)

BETH. Leeny?

MARLENE. Hi.

BETH. Hi.

(*They hug.*)

ARTHUR. You know, Carl Sandburg used to live in this area.

RON. No kidding?

ARTHUR. Yes. I believe so.

MARLENE. You look great.

BETH. I feel great.

MARLENE. You're happy.

BETH. I am so happy. You wouldn't have believed it. He walked into the library, asked me for the latest copy of the Journal of Conflict Resolution and I was in heaven.

After that, he came in everyday for a month and here we are. All those little cupcakes, pushing their little carts around, all those little Parker Poseys, they're eating their hearts out.

MARLENE. That's great.

BETH. So you've got to come down and meet him.

MARLENE. Okay.

(MARLENE reaches towards her suitcase.)

BETH. You. Just you.

MARLENE. Okay.

(MARLENE doesn't move.)

RON. Did you know Muhammed Ali has a house nearby?

ARTHUR. I didn't know.

RON. Yeah. It's for sale if you want to go take a look at it.

ARTHUR. I'll keep that in mind.

BETH. Leeny, come on. You can do this. He's waiting for you.

MARLENE. Okay.

(MARLENE walks to the door, but she doesn't go through it.)

ARTHUR. I'm looking forward to meeting her.

RON. Yeah. In a minute, you'll meet her and Lily.

ARTHUR. Lily is the dummy?

RON. We say, "ventriloquist's doll." She finds it helps her in social situations. Once she meets you one on one, she'll be okay.

(BETH walks back into the bedroom.)

BETH. Leeny, you didn't come to my wedding. Now I want you to come meet my husband.

MARLENE. I'll be down in a minute.

ARTHUR. I'm not going to talk to a doll.

BETH. Just you.

MARLENE. I'll be down in a minute.

RON. When she says something to you, you just respond.

(**BETH** *exits the Green Room.*)

ARTHUR. I'm not going to have a conversation with an inanimate object.

RON. You will. You'll see.

(**BETH** *comes back downstairs.*)

Is she coming?

BETH. No.

RON. I'll go get her.

(**RON** *goes upstairs.* **BETH** *turns to* **ARTHUR.**)

BETH. Can we go now?

ARTHUR. You know what Ron just told me?

BETH. What?

(**RON** *enters his room.*)

ARTHUR.	**RON.**
"Muhammed Ali has a house near here?"	Hey. Will you come say hi?

BETH.	**MARLENE.**
I'm sorry.	Okay.

(*She doesn't move.*)

ARTHUR. Let's make the black guy feel at home. "It's okay, Black Man. You're actually not the only black man for miles around."

BETH. Actually, I think you are.

RON. Arthur's looking forward to meeting you and Lily.

MARLENE. Really?

RON. He said so.

MARLENE. We'll be down in a minute.

RON. Good.

(**RON** *exits and comes down stairs. At the same time,* **DYLAN** *enters from the basement, distraught.*)

DYLAN. There's no cable.

BETH. What, Honey?

DYLAN. There's no cable! There's, like, two stations!

BETH. Well, Honey / Nobody's here often enough.

DYLAN. There's, like, fuzz! And The Berenstain Bears!

BETH. Honey, this is our time to be together.

DYLAN. With no TV?!

BETH. There's a sports bar in town, I–

DYLAN. Sports bar?! Do I look like I play sports?!

ARTHUR.	**BETH.**
Dylan.	Honey...

DYLAN. What?!

ARTHUR. I think we can discuss this like mature individuals.

BETH. Maybe we can get cable service for the week–

DYLAN. You can't get cable service for a week!

DYLAN.	**BETH.** *(sings)*
You have to order it! And then you have to wait for the cable guy to come and install it! Just that can take a week. *(calming down)* You don't even have a DVD player. Or a VCR.	GETTING TO KNOW YOU GETTING TO KNOW ALL ABOUT YOU GETTING TO LIKE YOU GETTING TO HOPE YOU LIKE ME.

(DYLAN stops.)

RON. That was interesting.

BETH. It's a new technique my therapist gave me. The idea is when we fall into our old destructive patterns, we sing to divert the energy to another path. It's called Flood Control.

DYLAN. Where's my room?

BETH. You're in the Blue Room. Upstairs.

(DYLAN walks over to the steps just as MARLENE comes downstairs with LILY, MARLENE's doll. DYLAN and LILY see each other.)

DYLAN.	LILY.
(caught off guard)	*(screams)*
Ahhhh!	Ahhhhhhhhhhhhhhh!

MARLENE. *(to LILY)* It's okay. It's okay.

(LILY *checks out* DYLAN.)

LILY. Well...What do we have here?

(to MARLENE) He's hot!

MARLENE. Be nice.

LILY. *(to DYLAN)* I'm here all week. How 'bout you?

DYLAN. Mommy?

BETH. It's okay, Honey. You can go to your room.

(DYLAN *goes upstairs.*)

LILY. *(to DYLAN, as he goes)* See ya'.

(DYLAN *finds his room, puts on his iPod, and flops down on the bed.*)

(RON *goes to* MARLENE *and* LILY *and brings them over to meet* ARTHUR.)

RON. Marlene. Lily. I'd like you to meet Beth's husband, Arthur.

LILY. Well...What do we have here?

ARTHUR. Marlene, it's nice to meet you.

MARLENE. You, too.

LILY. He's hot!

MARLENE. Lily.

ARTHUR. *(to BETH)* That's very clever.

LILY. *(to ARTHUR)* Say it loud, I'm Black and I'm hot!

MARLENE. Lily.

ARTHUR. *(to MARLENE)* How long have you been doing this?

LILY. *(to MARLENE)* He's so handsome.

MARLENE. Yes, he is.

LILY. *(to ARTHUR)* What immortal hand or eye could frame thy fearful symmetry?

(ARTHUR *laughs.*)

ARTHUR. Well, I never thought I'd hear a doll recite William Blake.

LILY. You like William Blake?

ARTHUR. Oh my, yes.

LILY. Do you know this one? "O the cunning wiles that creep / In thy little heart asleep."

(**ARTHUR** *joins in.*)

LILY & ARTHUR. *(in unison)* "When thy little heart doth wake / Then the dreadful night shall break."

LILY. *(cheers)* Yayyyy!

(*to* **ARTHUR**)

How do you like Walt Whitman?

ARTHUR. Walt Whitman? Oh, well–

ARTHUR.	**RON.**
It's very interesting that you say that.	Arthur.

RON. *(louder)* Arthur.

(**ARTHUR** *turns to* **RON**.)

ARTHUR. What?

RON. You're talking to the doll.

(**ARTHUR** *realizes that he's been had. He laughs good-naturedly.*)

ARTHUR. Okay, well, you got me there. That's very good.

LILY. *(to* **MARLENE**) Smart guy.

MARLENE. Be nice.

ARTHUR. *(to* **LILY**) Well, Lily...

LILY. I'm here all week. How 'bout you?

ARTHUR. Yes. Me, too. I hope we'll have a chance to get to know each other.

LILY. Me, too.

ARTHUR. All of us.

MARLENE. Me, too.

(*to* **LILY**) Let's go.

LILY. Go? We just got here.

MARLENE. You'll see him later.

(**MARLENE** *takes* **LILY** *and turns to go.* **LILY** *turns back to* **ARTHUR.**)

LILY. See ya' later.

ARTHUR. See you later.

(**MARLENE** *goes back upstairs to her room. As she goes,* **LILY** *keeps talking to* **ARTHUR.**)

LILY. Maybe tonight...Sometimes, I walk in my sleep...At two o'clock...In the kitchen...

(**MARLENE** *takes* **LILY** *into her room.*)

ARTHUR. She should be on Letterman.

RON. Why don't you show Arthur around? I'll bring in your stuff.

(**RON** *goes outside.*)

BETH. Come on. I'll give you the dime tour. This is the living room.

ARTHUR. Excellent.

(*She leads him to the back porch.*)

BETH. If you go out through here, that path takes you down to the beach.

(*Fifi, the dog, barks offstage.*)

Ohmigod. They brought the dog.

ARTHUR. Is that bad?

BETH. I hate that thing. What they spend on that dog, I could send Dylan to college. *(sighing)* If only we could have the house to ourselves.

ARTHUR. Any chance of that?

BETH. Not this week.

(*She continues the tour.*)

Here's the kitchen.

(*She leads him upstairs.*)

(**JAN** *enters from the basement, carrying a box.*)

JAN. I can't believe how much crap is down there. What are we supposed to do with all of this?

(She goes back downstairs.)

*(***BETH*** *knocks on the door of the Green Room.)*

MARLENE. Yes?

*(***BETH*** *opens the door.)*

BETH. May we come in?

MARLENE. Sure.

*(***BETH*** *and* ***ARTHUR*** *enter.)*

BETH. This is the Green Room.

ARTHUR. *(to* **MARLENE***)* Hello again.

MARLENE. Hi.

*(***MARLENE*** *and* ***LILY*** *wave.* ***BETH*** *shoves* ***ARTHUR*** *out and closes the door behind her. They go to the Blue Room and open the door.)*

BETH. This is the Blue Room.

(to **DYLAN***)* Honey, you doing okay?

*(***DYLAN*** *closes the door.* ***BETH*** *leands* ***ARTHUR*** *to the parent's room.)*

This is my parents' room. Where we should be staying. I don't even want to be in here.

(She leads him back downstairs.)

ARTHUR. So, all told, the house could accommodate eight? Maybe ten?

BETH. Maybe.

ARTHUR. It's perfect. It's even better than you described.

(She leads him into the Gold Room.)

BETH. And this is the Gold Room. With twin beds. I'm sorry.

ARTHUR. We'll be fine.

*(***RON*** *comes in, carrying luggage, and goes to the Gold Room. He knocks.)*

RON. May I come in?

BETH. Yes.

(**RON** *enters.*)

RON. Where should I put this?

BETH. Anywhere.

RON. And you want that big, red suitcase?

BETH. Yes, please.

RON. And the duffel bag is Dylan's?

BETH. Yes. Thank you.

RON. No problem.

(**RON** *exits and goes back outside.*)

BETH. *(to* **ARTHUR***)* Why don't we drive over to Union Pier? I know a nice little B and B.

ARTHUR. You have to be here.

BETH. I know. Don't leave me.

ARTHUR. I'm not going to leave you.

(*They embrace.*)

(**JAN** *comes back up from the basement, carrying a box, followed by* **YOUSEF***, carrying a box.*)

JAN. *(to* **YOUSEF***)* Will you go to the store already? I'm dying here.

(**YOUSEF** *goes over and looks at the list.*)

YOUSEF. There's nothing here from Beth.

JAN. *(calling)* Beth!

BETH. *(calling)* What?!

JAN. Joe's going to the store!

BETH. *(to* **ARTHUR***)* Do you want anything?

ARTHUR. Whatever you want. What do you want?

BETH. Privacy.

ARTHUR. I'll go add it to the list.

(**ARTHUR** *enters and goes to the shopping list.* **JAN** *goes back to the basement.*)

YOUSEF. Put down anything you want. I'll get it.

ARTHUR. Thank you.

YOUSEF. Later, you can pay me.

ARTHUR. Right.

(He sits down and writes.)

This is a great house.

YOUSEF. Oh, yes.

ARTHUR. It's great for Beth to have some peace and quiet.

YOUSEF. Peace and quiet? She works in a library.

ARTHUR. There's a lot of stress involved. People don't realize.

YOUSEF. Oh, yes. All those...books.

ARTHUR. Absolutely.

(Pause)

So what do you think they're going to do with it?

YOUSEF. I don't know.

ARTHUR. Has Jan indicated any–

YOUSEF. I don't know.

*(**ARTHUR** finishes writing. He hands the list to **YOUSEF**.)*

ARTHUR. Okay. I think that'll do it for now.

YOUSEF. Okay.

ARTHUR. Okay.

(Pause.)

YOUSEF. Want to see my car?

ARTHUR. Uh...Okay.

(They exit out the back way.)

YOUSEF. *(as they go)* It's a 6.2 liter, V8 engine. I got room for six, seven, even eight people...

*(**RON** has entered, carrying a suitcase and a duffel bag. He leaves the suitcase and takes the duffel bag up to the Blue Room. He knocks and enters.)*

RON. Hey. This is yours?

(DYLAN doesn't respond. RON drops the duffel bag. DYLAN removes his headphones.)

Hey.

DYLAN. Hey.

RON. I just wanted to tell you. All this week. You be nice to your mother.

DYLAN. What is that? A threat?

RON. Hey. I'm an Assistant State's Attorney. I put people in jail for a living.

(RON exits. DYLAN replaces his headphones.)

(RON goes downstairs, picks up the suitcase, and takes it to the Gold Room. He knocks.)

BETH. Yes?

(RON opens the door.)

RON. May I come in?

BETH. Sure.

(RON enters and drops the suitcase.)

RON. Here you go.

BETH. Thank you.

(RON closes the door.)

RON. Hi.

BETH. Hi.

(He goes to her and puts his arms around her.)

RON. Oh, God, I've missed you.

BETH. Oh, Ron.

RON. I miss you so much.

BETH. Ron.

(She starts to push him away.)

No. No.

(He resists.)

RON. Yes. Yes.

(DYLAN reaches into his pocket and removes his cell phone. He gets up and moves about the room, holding his cell phone up in the air.)

BETH. Ron. It's different now.

RON. What's different?

BETH. I'm different.

RON. Not to me. You still drive me crazy.

(DYLAN runs out of his room and runs out the front door.)

BETH. Oh, Ron.

RON. Meet me at the beach tonight.

BETH. I can't.

RON. Neither can I. Meet me at the beach tonight.

BETH. I can't.

RON. We'll be Burt Lancaster and Deborah Kerr in *From Here to Eternity*.

BETH. Ron.

RON. I'll let you be Burt Lancaster.

(DYLAN runs in, runs through the main room, and runs out the back door.)

BETH. Ron. What we had before…was before.

RON. We can have it again.

BETH. I'm married to Arthur now.

RON. I wish you years of happiness.

BETH. Thank you.

RON. Starting next week.

(DYLAN runs in and runs upstairs, trying to reach higher ground. He is frantic.)

DYLAN. Oh, God.

(BETH becomes aware of DYLAN's voice.)

BETH. *(to RON)* Just a second.

(She goes out the door. RON follows.)

DYLAN. Oh, God!

BETH. Dylan?

DYLAN. Oh, God!

(YOUSEF enters, followed by ARTHUR.)

YOUSEF. What is going on?

BETH. Honey, what is it?

DYLAN. I can't get a signal!

BETH. On your cell phone?

RON. *(to DYLAN)* You want to try mine?

(RON gives his cell phone to DYLAN.)

ARTHUR. This side of the lake, it's probably -

DYLAN. *(looking at the display)* Nothing!

BETH. *(to ARTHUR)* Arthur, can we try yours?

ARTHUR. I didn't bring mine. I'm on vacation.

BETH. Maybe mine will –

(She runs into her room.)

DYLAN. Who'm I going to talk to?

ARTHUR. There are lots of people around. / I'm sure if you want to...

DYLAN. I need to talk to my people.

(BETH comes out of her room, holding her cell phone.)

BETH. Mine's not working either.

DYLAN. I'm on the dark side of the moon!

BETH. *(to YOUSEF)* Joe, you must have the latest thing.

YOUSEF. Oh, yes.

BETH. Can Dylan borrow it?

YOUSEF. Eh...No. I need it.

DYLAN. *(to BETH)* Where's a computer?

BETH. Uh... There's no computer here.

DYLAN. *(ballistic)* What?!

DYLAN.	**BETH.**
There's no computer?!	We've never had a computer here.

DYLAN. I can't get online?!

BETH. I don't know. Maybe–

DYLAN. How'm I gonna charge my iPod?

BETH. Don't you have batteries?

DYLAN. No, I don't have batteries! I need a USB port!

BETH. I don't think we have one.

DYLAN. No, you don't have one if you don't have a computer!

BETH. I'm sorry.

DYLAN. Why did you bring me here?!

BETH. I'm sorry.

DYLAN. I hate it here! This is hell!

(**JAN** *enters with another box.*)

JAN. What a load of junk.

DYLAN.	**BETH.** *(singing through her tears)*
Why did you bring me here? This is hell!	WHAT GOOD IS SITTING ALONE IN YOUR ROOM
JAN. *(to* **YOUSEF***)* What's going on?	COME HEAR THE MUSIC PLAY LIFE IS A CABARET OLD CHUM
DYLAN.	COME TO THE CABARET.
I've got to get out of here!	PUT DOWN THE KNITTING
Why did you bring me here?!	THE BOOK AND THE BROOM
This is hell!!!	TIME FOR A HOLIDAY
	LIFE IS A CABARET OLD CHUM...

(fade out)

End of Scene 1.

SCENE 2

*(AT RISE: **YOUSEF** is sitting at the table, reading a newspaper and drinking coffee. **ARTHUR** enters from the Gold Room.)*

ARTHUR. Good morning, my friend.

*(**YOUSEF** looks around to see who **ARTHUR** is talking to. He realizes **ARTHUR** is talking to him.)*

YOUSEF. Oh. Hello. How are you? Would you like some coffee?

ARTHUR. Oh, yes. I'd love some.

*(**YOUSEF** rises and goes to get a cup of coffee. **ARTHUR** sits at the table.)*

Any plans for the day?

YOUSEF. I don't know.

ARTHUR. Looks like a beautiful day.

*(**BETH** comes up from the basement with a box of stuff, puts it on the counter and comes over to **ARTHUR**.)*

Good morning, my dear.

BETH. Good morning.

*(**BETH** goes back down to the basement. **YOUSEF** gives **ARTHUR** a cup of coffee.)*

YOUSEF. Here you go.

ARTHUR. Ah, thank you. That looks great.

*(**ARTHUR** takes a sip and it is not anywhere near to his taste.)*

Wow...That's, uh...That's...What is that?

YOUSEF. That is Persian coffee.

ARTHUR. That's, uh...That's really something.

YOUSEF. Thank you.

*(**ARTHUR** covertly gets rid of the coffee as he makes conversation.)*

ARTHUR. So...What do you think they should do with this place?

YOUSEF. I don't know.

ARTHUR. It's so peaceful here. I understand they used to spend all summer up here.

YOUSEF. Oh, yes.

ARTHUR. But since their mother passed away...

YOUSEF. With the father, we would come for one week only.

ARTHUR. So, Yousef...You get along with all these white people?

YOUSEF. They're not white. They're Jews.

ARTHUR. *(understanding)* Ah...What happened when Jan brought you home to meet the parents?

YOUSEF. The mother thought I was Jewish because I don't eat pork.

ARTHUR. *(smiling)* Oh, you must have enjoyed that.

YOUSEF. No.

ARTHUR. But, ultimately, you managed–

YOUSEF. The father was not so easy. The mother was okay. The mother you could talk to. But then the mother had a heart attack and died so you couldn't talk to her anymore.

ARTHUR. But she was okay with her daughter marrying an Arab.

YOUSEF. I'm not Arab. I'm Persian.

ARTHUR. Of course. Sorry.

> *(beat)*
>
> I'm black.

YOUSEF. I know.

ARTHUR. And here we are with the Jews. How about that?

YOUSEF. I like Jews. They're tough, but honest. You know Sam Zell?

ARTHUR. I know of him, but, no, not–

YOUSEF. He's a funny guy. He told me this one.

> *(quoting)*
>
> "Two Jews walk into a bar."

(BETH comes up from the basement with another box.)

ARTHUR. Yes, yes. I'm sure they do. I'm just going to...

YOUSEF. Okay.

(ARTHUR gets up.)

ARTHUR. Thank you for the, uh...

(He goes over to BETH.)

Find anything of interest?

BETH. Not yet.

ARTHUR. See if you can find some coffee.

BETH. *(referring to YOUSEF)* Did he...?

ARTHUR. Yes.

BETH. That's just cruel.

ARTHUR. I didn't hear you get up.

BETH. I couldn't sleep.

ARTHUR. You'll be all right. Have you had any breakfast?

BETH. No. No, I'm fine. I want to do this. I thought I would separate the physical objects from the paper items, group those into subsets of what could be categorized as memorabilia and what is obviously discards, and then see what we've got.

ARTHUR. I marvel at your organizational skills.

(switching) Did you talk to your sisters yet?

BETH. No. I don't know if they're going to go for it.

ARTHUR. *(encouraging)* You have to be positive.

BETH. I am. I'm positive they're not going to go for it.

(Outside, FIFI barks.)

RON. *(offstage)* Get down!...Down!...Get...!

(RON enters, sweaty from a morning jog.)

RON. *(to YOUSEF)* Good morning.

YOUSEF. Good morning. How are you? Would you like some coffee?

RON. No. Thank you.

(to BETH and ARTHUR) Good morning.

*(**RON** goes over to the refrigerator, opens it, and is unhappy.)*

RON. *(to **YOUSEF**)* What is this?

YOUSEF. What?

*(**RON** holds up six-pack of Diet Rite.)*

RON. *(to **YOUSEF**)* This is Diet Rite.

YOUSEF. That is Diet Rite.

RON. I asked for Diet Coke.

YOUSEF. Same thing.

RON. It is not the– *(to **ARTHUR**)* Hey, Art!

ARTHUR. *(correcting him)* Arthur.

RON. Didn't you ask for Diet Coke?

ARTHUR. Yes.

RON. Well, they got Diet Rite.

ARTHUR. What?

*(**ARTHUR** goes to the kitchen.)*

RON. They got Diet Rite.

YOUSEF. It was on sale.

RON. Diet Rite is always on sale.

YOUSEF. It's the same thing.

RON. *(to **ARTHUR**)* You want to tell him?

ARTHUR. It is not the same thing. There is a world of difference–

RON. World of difference.

ARTHUR. Between Diet Rite and Diet Coke.

YOUSEF. All right. I will go to the store. I will get Diet Coke. Diet Coke. Diet Coke.

RON. And you should check the dog. I think her foot is bleeding.

YOUSEF. Sonuvabitch.

*(**YOUSEF** exits out the back.)*

RON. *(to **ARTHUR**, rhetorically)* Do you believe this guy?

ARTHUR. Oh, I don't think he did it intentionally.

RON. Oh, yes, he did. They do that kind of stuff. They only care about what they want. I wish you were Korean.

ARTHUR. Do you.

RON. Yeah. Then we could have dog for dinner.

ARTHUR. You have a real problem with that dog.

RON. That dog is an anti-semite. They breed them that way.

ARTHUR.	**BETH.**
Oh, I don't think -	Ron...

RON. No, it's true. That dog has been trained by Nazis.

ARTHUR. It's just a little French Poodle.

RON. French, right. You never heard of the Vichy Government?

ARTHUR. Yes, I've heard of the Vichy Government.

RON. And you know what's going on in France today? They train those dogs to hate Jews.

BETH. Ron, stop.

(*YOUSEF enters.*)

YOUSEF. The dog's okay.

RON. Oh, well, that's a relief.

YOUSEF. It wasn't blood. It's nail polish. Once a month, Jan takes her to a salon for haircut and manicure.

RON. Oh, of course.

ARTHUR. Of course. That's what I would do.

RON. Of course.

(*RON starts to go.*)

I'm going to hit the showers.

(*RON goes upstairs. JAN comes downstairs.*)

JAN. Good morning.

YOUSEF. Good morning. Do you want some coffee?

JAN. Yes. Please.

ARTHUR. *(to JAN)* Good morning.

JAN. Good morning. Did you sleep all right?

ARTHUR. Oh, yes.

BETH. In separate beds.

(**YOUSEF** *gives a cup of coffee to* **JAN**.)

JAN. Thank you.

ARTHUR. Careful. That's really...

(**JAN** *takes a sip.*)

JAN. Mmmm. Perfect.

ARTHUR. *(to* **BETH***)* Well, I think I'll go outside and commune with nature if that's all right with you.

BETH. Can you check in on Dylan?

ARTHUR. Oh, of course. I should have thought of that.

BETH. Maybe he'd like to go to the beach.

ARTHUR. Sure.

(**ARTHUR** *goes up to* **DYLAN***'s room.*)

YOUSEF. *(to* **JAN***)* I have to go out and get Diet Coke.

JAN. What's the matter with–

YOUSEF. I don't know.

(*They kiss and* **YOUSEF** *exits.*)

(**ARTHUR** *knocks on* **DYLAN***'s door.*)

DYLAN. What?!

(**ARTHUR** *opens the door and enters.*)

ARTHUR. May I come in?

DYLAN. *(defensively)* I'm not doing anything.

ARTHUR. I know. I know. That's cool. I was just wondering... It's a beautiful day. I'm heading down to the beach. Want to come along?

DYLAN. Down to the beach? Sure. It's one of my ambitions in life to get skin cancer.

ARTHUR. I'm sure your mom has some sunscreen.

DYLAN. I'm sure you're sure.

ARTHUR. Okay. I get it. You're not going to make this easy on me. But, you know, I have quite a bit of experience with angry young men. If you're willing to meet me halfway–

DYLAN. I'm not.

ARTHUR. You're just going to stay in here all week?

DYLAN. Looks like it.

ARTHUR. Then it's you who's missing out. There's a lot of good shit out there.

DYLAN. "Good shit?"

ARTHUR. Okay. I'll be more specific.

(*quoting*)

"If you can fill the unforgiving minute
With sixty seconds worth of distance run.
Yours is the earth and everything that's in it
And - Which is more - You'll be a man, my son."
That's Rudyard Kipling.

DYLAN. (*quoting*)

"Excuse me, is you saying something?
Uh, uh. You can't tell me nothing."
That's Kanye West.

ARTHUR. Okay. Well…You can think about it…And get back to me.

(**ARTHUR** *exits and goes back downstairs.*)

BETH. Is he coming?

ARTHUR. Oh, yes. I think so. In a while. We're going to be fine.

BETH. Oh, that's great, Sweetheart. Thank you.

ARTHUR. I'll be outside if you need me.

BETH. I'll be okay. Thank you.

(**ARTHUR** *exits out the back porch.*)

JAN. (*to* **BETH**) Are you going out?

BETH. Maybe later.

JAN. What are you bothering with that junk for?

BETH. I just want to see what's here.

(*She points to one box.*)

BETH. I found a bunch of letters in there.

JAN. Letters?

BETH. To Dad. From when we were still living in Rogers Park. There's no return address. Maybe they're love letters.

JAN. Love letters? To Dad? From who?

BETH. I don't know. I said maybe. I haven't read them yet.

JAN. Dad? No.

BETH. You never saw "Bridges of Madison County?"

JAN. Even if it were true...Would you want to know Dad had some great love affair at this point? Well, maybe you would. No. There was no "Bridges of Madison County" in Dad's life. Our father did not have a secret life. Dentists do not have secret lives.

BETH. McTeague.

JAN. What's McTeague?

BETH. McTeague is a dentist. Who has a secret life. In a novel by Frank Norris.

(BETH holds up a framed picture and displays it for JAN.)

BETH. Have you ever seen this picture?

JAN. Let me see.

(JAN looks at the picture.)

JAN. Uh...No.

BETH. Who's that with Dad?

JAN. I have no idea.

BETH. Maybe this is a special picture.

JAN. No. The picture of Mom and Dad with Harry Belafonte. That was special. That was hanging in the living room. This is in a box in the basement in Michigan.

BETH. But why is it in a box in the basement in Michigan? Who is this guy?

JAN. Okay, now you're getting into "Brokeback Mountain" and I'm not even going to talk to you. Let's just get rid of this junk.

BETH. I just want to go through it. I'm not asking you to do it.

JAN. You can't see the forest for the trees. That's / always been your problem.

BETH. Yes, I can.

JAN. It's a waste of time.

BETH. We'll see.

JAN. *(calling out)* Beth! The forest! The forest!

BETH. Am I asking you to help?

JAN. No.

BETH. Then leave me alone. You didn't help clean out the Highland Park house, I / don't expect you to help clean out here.

JAN. I didn't help clean out the Highland Park house? I most certainly did help to clean out the / Highland Park house.

BETH. Jan...You were there for ten minutes. Just long enough to claim Mom's good silver / and then you left.

JAN. I was there for a week.

BETH. While we were sitting shiva. Then Marlene and I were there for another week.

JAN. I know I was there.

BETH. No, you weren't.

JAN. I did more than just take the silver.

BETH. *(remembering)* Oh! Yes! That's right! You took the Lexus, too.

JAN. Dad had already promised that to Sammy.

BETH. When?

JAN. When he was in the hospital.

BETH. You were never in the hospital!

JAN. I most certainly / was in the hospital.

BETH. For an hour. For maybe one hour.

JAN. Well, I can't stand hospitals. All those sick people.

BETH. Well, I'm sorry we couldn't arrange to have Dad's surgery in the rec room.

JAN. "Rec room?"

BETH.	**JAN.**
Of course, if we had, you wouldn't have been there to help clean it up.	"Rec room?" What are you, nine? We haven't had a rec room since we lived in Lincolnwood.

(**MARLENE** *enters through the front door.*)

MARLENE. It's a beautiful day outside.

(**BETH** *calls to* **MARLENE**.)

BETH. Did Jan come to the house in Highland Park?

MARLENE. Yeah. Lots of times.

BETH. After Dad died?

MARLENE. Oh, well...

BETH. *(to* **JAN***, triumphant)* See?

JAN. I was there plenty of times.

(**BETH** *picks up the photo and shows it to* **MARLENE**.)

BETH. Do you know who this is?

MARLENE. That's Dad.

BETH. No. The other guy.

MARLENE. Mmmm...I don't know.

JAN. *(calling out)* Beth! The forest! The forest!

(**MARLENE** *removes a shoe box from one of the boxes.*)

MARLENE. What is this?

BETH. I don't know.

(**MARLENE** *opens the box and removes one shoe.*)

MARLENE. It's a shoe.

JAN. *(with mock amazement)* Imagine that. You open up a shoe box and there's a shoe in it.

MARLENE. It's black patent leather. Do you suppose this was Dad's?

BETH. It couldn't be. It's huge.

MARLENE. Would you like this?

BETH. What am I going to do with one shoe?

MARLENE. I don't know. I guess we could donate it somewhere.

BETH. Why would somebody donate one shoe?

MARLENE. I don't know. There must be some needy one-legged people.

BETH. Needy one-legged people? Going to a formal event?

MARLENE. Maybe.

(**MARLENE** *looks in the big box.*)

Maybe the other shoe is in here.

(*She stops.*)

Oh, my god.

BETH. What?

(**MARLENE** *removes a binder from the box.*)

MARLENE. This is my stamp collection.

BETH. I remember that.

(**MARLENE** *opens it up and peruses the pages.*)

MARLENE. Oh, my god.

BETH. The two of you used to hole up for hours with that thing.

MARLENE. I'd like to keep this. If that's all right.

BETH. You know what? Actually…I'd love to give it to Dylan. He doesn't have anything of his grandfather's and I'm desperate to find something that might interest him. Can I have it please? For Dylan?

MARLENE. I'd really like to have it.

BETH. It's not like you were looking for it. It'll just end up back in the basement.

MARLENE. No, it won't. I love these. They're beautiful.

BETH. What are you going to do with it?

MARLENE. I'll take care of it.

BETH. Dylan will take care of it. He would respect this. I bet some of some of these are worth a lot of money.

MARLENE. They are.

JAN. They are?

MARLENE. Yes. There are some very valuable stamps here.

(**JAN** *comes over.*)

JAN. Like what?

MARLENE. There's a lot of them.

(**MARLENE** *points to one stamp.*)

See this one? With George Washington on it? That's from 1928.

JAN. How much is that worth?

MARLENE. I don't know. In today's market. A few hundred, at least.

JAN. A few hundred?

(**MARLENE** *points to another part of the page.*)

MARLENE. And this. This is a set from 1930. In mint condition, this is worth, I bet, at least, a thousand dollars.

JAN. All right. I'm taking this.

MARLENE. What?

BETH. No, you're not.

JAN. We need to get this appraised. This is part of Dad's estate.

BETH. No, it's not.

JAN. I'm the executor of the estate. I say what we're going to do with this.

BETH. Look, your kid got the Lexus. How about Dylan gets the stamps?

MARLENE. I would like to have it. It's something I shared with Dad.

BETH. And it really meant a lot to you.

MARLENE. It did.

JAN. Then why was it sitting in the basement?

BETH. Yeah.

MARLENE. I gave it to him after Mom was gone. He was just sitting around. It gave him something to do.

JAN. So you gave it to him.

BETH. Then it's not really yours.

JAN. It's Dad's. It's part of the estate.

MARLENE. I would just like to have it.

BETH. So would I.

JAN. Nobody's doing anything until I get this appraised.

BETH. Will you relax? It's not worth all that much.

MARLENE. It's just sentimental.

JAN. Yeah. It's very easy to get sentimental about something you don't want someone else to have.

MARLENE. You don't want it.

BETH. But I do.

JAN. Just because you're sentimental about the stamps doesn't mean you get the stamps.

MARLENE. Okay.

JAN. That's right.

MARLENE. Okay.

JAN. Next thing you're going to say is you have sentimental feelings about the house.

MARLENE. I do.

BETH & JAN. What?

MARLENE. I do. I do have sentimental feelings about the house. Don't you?

(**JAN** *and* **BETH** *look at each other and then both turn on* **MARLENE.**)

JAN. Marlene. / That's very sweet.

BETH. Leeny, look. I have sentimental feelings / about the house, of course I do.

JAN. But we really need to be rational / about this. There are practical matters.

BETH. But we're not kids anymore. We can't just let things go like they used to.

MARLENE. Why not?!

(That stops **JAN** *and* **BETH**.*)*

Look, Dad had plenty of time to put his affairs in order. Everything was spelled out to a T. But in the will, he left out the house. Why would he do that? I think he didn't put the house in the will because he wanted us to keep it in the family.

JAN. No. Leeny, I'm sorry. He didn't put it in the will because he didn't give a shit.

MARLENE. He loved it here.

JAN. Mom loved it. He didn't love it.

BETH. He only came up here to make Mom happy.

MARLENE. But after she was gone, he -

BETH. He came up here to make us happy.

MARLENE. I thought we came here to make him happy.

JAN. And now we don't have to do that anymore.

MARLENE. You don't want to hold onto the place just for old times sake?

JAN. Even if we did, it doesn't make any sense. There's no point in letting the house sit here if you're only using it one week out of the year. You have to pay taxes, you have to–

MARLENE. How much are the taxes?

JAN. See, you don't even know how much the taxes are.

BETH. How much are they?

JAN. I don't know. The bill goes to Barry, the lawyer. He pays it out of the estate account. But it has to be ten, fifteen grand a year.

BETH. Really?

JAN. You could cover that with rentals, but -

BETH.	**MARLENE.**
No!	No rentals!

BETH. We promised Mom.

JAN. I know.

> *(imitating Mom)* "I don't want strangers in my house." So no rentals. Leeny. We need to be rational about this. It just doesn't make sense for the house to just sit here. So–

BETH. So...The best solution would be to keep the house in the family, but find a way to make use of it so it doesn't just sit here. Then everybody'd be happy.

JAN. There's no way–

BETH. Well...Arthur and I have been talking and here's the plan. We put just a little money into the place to fix it up a little bit. And we can probably get the money through a grant from the state's arts council. And then, during the summer months when Arthur is off from school, we establish an artist's colony like Ragdale and it'd be wonderful. We could establish ourselves as a non-profit organization so we would get a break on taxes. You charge a fee to cover food and maintenance and stuff so all your running costs are offset. We would call it the Levy Center for the Arts. Mom would love that. We could get writers and artists from Chicago and Michigan and Arthur and I and maybe Dylan would be here so we'd keep an eye on everyone and we'd be here so you could come up whenever you want.

> **(BETH** *stops talking and waits for the response.)*

JAN. Are you out of your mind?

BETH. No.

JAN. A bunch of starving artists / in the house?

BETH. They're not starving.

JAN. They'd trash the place. In two weeks, the place would be gone.

BETH. No, it–

JAN. I'd rather have termites in the house. I'd rather have locusts. If the ten plagues of Egypt were visited upon the house, there wouldn't be as much damage.

BETH. You are so–

JAN. Beth. Beth. Beth. *(calming down)* It's a lovely idea. The Levy Center for the Arts.

(She chortles and then recovers.)

But it's not practical. We have to look at this rationally. Beth. Leeny. Please. As the elder of the family -

BETH. "Elder of the family?" Oh, please.

JAN. Well, I am. Now that Dad's gone.

BETH. Don't play the age card. You're two years older than me and three years older than her.

JAN. It's not just about years. I have the most life experience.

BETH. I have just as much life experience as you do.

JAN. The kind of life experience you have is not relevant to our situation.

BETH. *(warning)* Don't go there.

JAN. *(warning)* Don't make me go there.

BETH. If, for once in your life, you would take me seriously–

JAN. I will take you seriously when you start acting seriously. Now, enough of this. The only thing that makes sense is for us to sell the house.

BETH. But–

JAN. Believe me. With your share of the sale, you'll be able to feed a lot of starving artists.

(This gives **BETH** *pause.)*

BETH. Really?

JAN. Pick up a newspaper. Look at what houses go for in this area.

BETH. How much do you think we can get?

JAN. Four bedrooms, two baths? Beachfront property? Easily...Two million.

BETH. Two million dollars?

JAN. No. Sheckels. Of course, two million dollars.

BETH. And we split that evenly?

JAN. Even Steven. Three way split. After expenses.

BETH. What expenses?

JAN. Well, there might be closing costs. Commissions. Standard stuff.

BETH. Who gets the commission?

JAN. Well, I can't legally be the listing agent because I'm not licensed in Michigan. But I have a friend who works in the New Buffalo office. She'll be the listing agent, but she'll give me the commission. Call it a referral fee. It's perfectly legal.

BETH. So that's a nice chunk of change for you.

JAN. Somebody's got to get it.

BETH. Why?

JAN. That's how the real estate business works. What, you want somebody else to get the commission?

BETH. I don't want anybody to get the commission. Can't we–

JAN. When you sell a house, you have to pay a commission.

BETH. You said it would be an even split.

JAN. It will be.

BETH. After you take the commission.

JAN. That's right.

BETH. But you don't have to take a commission. You could -

JAN. It's what I do.

BETH. But you don't have to. You're taking money out of our pockets.

JAN. No, I'm not.

BETH. Yes, you are.

(*to* **MARLENE**) Would you say something?

MARLENE. I don't want to sell the house.

BETH. Oh, you're a big help.

JAN. If I come into your library and I want to check out a book and I don't have my library card, are you going to let me check out the book?

BETH. You? No.

JAN. Okay then.

BETH. What?

JAN. It's the same thing.

BETH. What is?

JAN. It's the same thing. You're not going to let me check out a book. I'm not going to give up my commission.

BETH. That's not the same thing.

JAN. Yes, / it is.

BETH. It's not the same thing. If I don't let you check out a book, I'm not taking money out / of your pocket.

JAN. I'm not taking money / out of your pocket.

BETH. If you take a commission on the sale of this house, you're taking money out of my pocket.

JAN. So you want me to give up my commission.

BETH. Yes.

JAN. Then you're taking money out of my pocket.

BETH. No, I'm / not.

JAN. Yes.

BETH. No.

JAN. Yes. *(to MARLENE)* Will you back me up on this?

MARLENE. I don't want to sell the house.

JAN. *(to BETH)* You don't understand the real estate business.

BETH. Look, I promised myself when I got here, I wasn't going to let you just take whatever you want.

JAN. I'm not.

BETH. Jan, excuse me. Whatever you want is always the most important thing without regard for other people's feelings.

JAN. That's the way it is with everybody.

BETH. No, it isn't. Some people put other people's needs ahead of their own.

JAN. Stupid people.

BETH. Oh, now I'm stupid.

JAN. When?

BETH. What?

JAN. When could it possibly be better to put somebody else's needs ahead of your own?

BETH. Oh, gee, I don't know. Let me think. Like, maybe, if I had a sister who was getting married, but I had a previous engagement–

JAN. Oh, that's what this is about.

BETH. That's just / one example.

JAN. I told you–

BETH. I know what you / told me.

JAN. If there's an awards dinner and you're the one getting the award, you have to show up.

BETH. "Broker of the Year" is not exactly the Pulitzer Prize.

JAN. Maybe it doesn't mean anything / to you, but–

BETH. Oh, come on. The only reason you got the award is because your husband paid for the dinner.

JAN. Everyone there paid five hundred dollars a plate. All Joe paid for was the room and the flowers.

BETH. And next he's going to pay for you to become an Alderman.

JAN. That is–

BETH. How else are you going to win?

JAN. I will be elected because I'm the best person for the job.

BETH. You're a Republican in Chicago! What chance do you have?

JAN.	MARLENE.
I don't need this.	Guys.

BETH. I'm not selling the house just so you can have a big payday.

JAN. Just because I didn't come to your wedding?

BETH. You didn't. Come. To my wedding.

JAN. All right! I'm sorry! I missed your wedding! Give me a break! I'm sorry! I'll come to the next one!

BETH. That is the most–

JAN. What? It's my fault?

BETH. How many times / I've been married is–

JAN. Elizabeth Taylor's got nothing on you.

BETH. Elizabeth Taylor's–

JAN. Floundering from / one man to the next.

BETH. Floundering! Just because you're life is perfect.

JAN. My life is not perfect.

BETH. You always get whatever you want. 'Cause you're the Queen.

JAN. I'm not the–

BETH. You've got the perfect life.

JAN. I do not–

BETH. You've got the perfect children.

(YOUSEF enters.)

You've got the perfect husband.

JAN. He's not perfect.

YOUSEF. I'm not?

BETH. Some of us have to work at being happy.

JAN. I work.

BETH. You–

JAN. I work! It's just / once I commit to something -

BETH. I don't commit?! I don't commit?!

JAN. You go through men like Kleenex!

BETH. *(referring to YOUSEF)* You picked him up in a bar!

JAN. I did not.

BETH. You always said you picked him up because you thought he looked like Prince.

JAN. He does not look like Prince.

YOUSEF. I don't?

BETH. You always get whatever you want.

JAN. Like you don't always get whatever you want.

BETH. When have I ever gotten / everything I want?

JAN. Oh, come on. I have to remind you?

BETH. When have I ever gotten–

JAN. You really want to–

BETH. When have I ever gotten everything I want?

JAN. Marty Klein.

(**MARLENE** *and* **YOUSEF** *groan.*)

BETH. *(incredulous)* What?

JAN. You heard me.

BETH. Marty Klein. That's ancient history.

JAN. That's what you wanted.

BETH. Marty Klein. I can't believe you're still pissed off about Marty Klein.

JAN. You wanted him, you got him.

BETH. That was in high school.

JAN. And how I felt about him was immaterial.

BETH. I can't believe–

JAN. So don't accuse me of getting what I want without regard for other people's feelings.

BETH. I'm not accusing you.

JAN. Did I say I want to sell the house and keep all the money to myself?

(**RON** *comes downstairs.*)

BETH.	**RON.**
(to **JAN***)* That is what you'd like to do, though, isn't it?	What the hell is going on down here? *(He goes to* **MARLENE.***)* *What's going on?*
JAN.	
No. Because I want to do something for other people.	
BETH.	**MARLENE.**
No. I want to do something for other people.	People are yelling.
JAN.	**RON.**
And what's in it for me?	*(trying to get their attention)* Hey!

BETH.

"What's in it for me."   Hey!
See, it's always about
what's in it for you.

JAN. No, it isn't. *(to* **YOUSEF***)* You want to talk to her?

YOUSEF. No.

RON. Hey! Why don't I get everyone a Xanax and we can sit down and discuss this like mature adults?

(**ARTHUR** *enters.*)

ARTHUR. I could hear you all the way–

JAN.	**BETH.**
(to **YOUSEF***)* I can't I can't talk to her.	It's hopeless. I can't I can't talk to her.
YOUSEF.	**ARTHUR.**
What is the problem?	Did you tell her–
JAN.	**BETH.**
They want the whole house for themselves. Forget about us. They want to turn the house into - I don't know - a camp. For… Writers… And artists.	Yes. And she instantly dismissed it. Unless there's a way for her to make money on it, she's not interested.
YOUSEF.	**ARTHUR.**
That's crazy.	Did you explain–
JAN.	**BETH.**
I know.	Yes! I told her the whole thing. I was calm. I was rational.

YOUSEF. *(calling)* Beth! Beth!

(**BETH** *turns to* **YOUSEF**.)

BETH. What?

YOUSEF. You're crazy.

BETH. Why is it crazy to want to do something for others?

JAN.
> For strangers. Why don't you worry about doing something for your own family?

BETH.
> What have you done for your own family lately? / It's not enough you get what you want. You take pleasure in the misfortune of others.

JAN.
> Look, if your life isn't The way you want it to be, maybe you should take some responsibility / instead of your "poor me, poor me."

BETH.
> You revel in it! It's Schadenfreude!

ARTHUR.
> I don't think you fully understand / the ramifications.

RON.
> Excuse me. / You've been part of this family for, what, like, ten minutes? This is the Levy House. The Levy House. You don't come into somebody else's house and tell them what to do with their house.

YOUSEF.
> What I don't understand is why / you would even consider such a thing.

ARTHUR.
> The advantages of a non-profit organization / are certainly worth exploring.

YOUSEF.
> Non-profit?...Non-profit?

ARTHUR.
> Well, come on. Money isn't everything.

YOUSEF.
> Oh, yes it is. This is America.

Schadenfreude!

(**DYLAN** *comes bounding down the stairs.*)

DYLAN. I got something to say and you really better listen.

There's sure a lot of noise in here and you should quit your bitchin.

I know I'm just a callow youth and all the world's a stage.

But I'm lookin' at the world now and I am in a rage.

There's brother versus brother and sister versus sister.

I'm not supposed to speak my mind but listen to me mister.

All the people in the streets are out there getting whacked.

The president's a maniac and that's the fact, Jack.

(MARLENE comes up behind DYLAN and adds a beatbox rhythm.)

The oceans and the air we breathe are choking from pollution.

The atmosphere is gone, I fear. I don't have the solution.

Pretty soon the planet will be just a pile of feces.

You hear what I am tellin' you? I'm the endangered species.

The only place I feel safe is Myspace online.

The Internet's a safety net where I can feel fine.

How'm I gonna find a way to live that's genuine?

The answer really isn't blowin' in the wind.

There's sister versus sister and brother versus brother.

You're blowin' up the world. Do you think I'll get another.

Stop the fightin', stop the war, and please stop all the killin'.

Everybody settle down! And save the world for Dylan.

(DYLAN brings his rap to a close and he and MARLENE stand, arms folded, gazing at the others.)

(Fade out)

End of Act One

ACT 2

Scene 1

*(At rise: **JAN** and **YOUSEF** are in the kitchen, making microwave popcorn. **MARLENE** is in her room, reading.)*

*(**ARTHUR** is in the living room, sitting on the couch. **RON**, in costume, is standing in the middle of the room.)*

RON. *(announcing)* Okay, come on, people! We've got to go in five minutes!

ARTHUR. I'm ready.

JAN. We'll be ready in a minute.

RON. You know, you can buy popcorn at the movie theatre.

JAN. *(dismissively)* Yeah.

YOUSEF. That's crazy.

JAN. Pay five bucks for a box of popcorn when we can make three boxes for two bucks?

RON. All right. Well...

   *(to **ARTHUR**)*

   Is Beth ready?

ARTHUR. I think so.

RON. Okay, well Art, Beth / and I are ready.

ARTHUR. Arthur.

RON. Why don't we just go in separate cars? / We can go ahead and save seats.

JAN. Oh, no.

JAN. We're going along with this little outing of yours, we're all going together.	**YOUSEF.** I have an Escalade ESV. It seats eight people so we can all go in my car.

JAN. *(cont.)*	YOUSEF. *(cont.)*
He bought that monster thing - The boys never use it. They have their own cars. So if we're all going to one place, we're all going in one car.	I haven't had eight people in it yet, but I'm sure we have enough room so we should use it. If we're all going to use our own cars, I would have brought the Lamborghini.

RON. All right. All right. But if we're going in your car, can I ride shotgun?

JAN. I don't care.

RON. And at the movie, I have to sit on the aisle, okay, because I have Restless Leg Syndrome, so...

(**ARTHUR** *comes over to the kitchen.*)

ARTHUR. Excuse me, Yousef.

YOUSEF. Yes. Hello. How are you?

ARTHUR. Good. Good. Listen, I was wondering... If we're all going in your car...could I drive?

YOUSEF. Ehhhhhh...No. Only I am the driver.

JAN. Joe and his cars.

   (rhetorically) What are you going to do?

   (to **ARTHUR***)* But I was going to tell you.

   (quoting) Two Jews walk into a bar...

RON. Can we move this along?

JAN. We'll be ready in a minute.

(Fifi barks offstage.)

(**BETH** *enters through the back door.*)

BETH. Hi.

ARTHUR. Hi.

BETH. Don't you look nice.

ARTHUR. I thought you were–

RON. *(to* **BETH***)* What are you doing?

BETH. I was on the beach.

RON. We're supposed to be going now.

BETH. Going where?

RON. We're going to "Sing-Along Mary Poppins."

BETH. *(sudden realization)* Is that tonight?

RON. Yes!

BETH. Well, nobody told me.

(She heads towards her room.)

RON. We've been talking about it for days. It's Jan's birthday.

BETH. Is that today?

JAN. Hello-o.

BETH. I'm sorry.

RON. *(to* **BETH***)* It's time to go.

BETH. Well, I have to rinse off.

RON. It's time to go!

BETH. Take me two minutes.

*(***BETH*** goes into her room.)*

RON. *(to* **JAN***)* Okay, are we ready?

JAN. In a minute. I just have to go put my face on.

*(***JAN*** heads upstairs.)*

RON. We're going to watch a movie. In the dark. What do you have to put your face on for?

JAN. There might be people there I know. What if I run into some of my constituents?

RON. Oh. You think you might see the people who are going to vote for you?

JAN. That's right.

*(***JAN*** exits into her rooom.)*

RON. Right.

(under his breath) They might both be there.

(calling to **JAN***)* Hurry up!

*(A cell phone rings. **YOUSEF** reaches into his pocket and removes his phone and answers it.)*

YOUSEF. *(into phone, in Farsi)* Salaam. Haaletoon chetoreh? Hameh chee khoob peesh meerah? Shomaa fahmeeded jalaseh kojag tashkeel meesheh? *(Translation: Hello. How are you? How's it going? Did you find out when the meeting is going to take place?)*

*(**YOUSEF** goes out the back door.)*

RON. *(to **ARTHUR**, referring to **YOUSEF**)* How 'bout that guy?

ARTHUR. Really.

RON. Drives a sixty thousand dollar car, but won't spend five bucks on a box of popcorn.

ARTHUR. Maybe that's why he can afford a sixty thousand dollar car.

*(referring to **RON**'s costume)* Who are you supposed to be anyway?

RON. I'm Uncle Albert.

ARTHUR. Isn't that from "Tommy?"

RON. No. That's Uncle Ernie. This is Ed Wynn as Uncle Albert in *Mary Poppins*. When they sing *I Love to Laugh*. Don't you remember?

ARTHUR. Well, I've never seen *Mary Poppins*.

RON. *(appalled)* You've never seen *Mary Poppins*?

ARTHUR. I read a couple of P.L. Travers' books in a Survey of Children's Literature course, but, no, I've never seen the film.

RON. It's not a "film." It's a movie. It's a great, big, singin' and dancin', supercalifragilisticexpealidocious movie. And when you see it with everybody singing along, that's the best.

ARTHUR. Well, I'm afraid I won't be able to sing along, I -

RON. No, that's all right.

*(**RON** reaches into his back pocket and removes some papers.)*

I printed up some lyric sheets for everybody so we can practice on the way there.

(**RON** *hands him the sheets.*)

ARTHUR. Thank you.

RON. I just have to run to the john.

(**RON** *goes upstairs.*)

I wanted to get there early to get good seats.

(**RON** *goes into the bathroom.* **ARTHUR** *looks at his lyric sheets.*)

ARTHUR. *(reading)* "Chim. Chi-MIN-ee. Chim. Chi-MIN-ee." Good lord.

(**JAN** *comes out of her room, limping because she has on one flat shoe and one high-heeled shoe. She goes to the Green Room and knocks.*)

JAN. Are you in there?

MARLENE. Yes.

(**JAN** *enters.*)

JAN. Leeny, help me. Which shoes should I wear?

MARLENE. Those are the choices?

JAN. Yeah, what do you think?

MARLENE. They're both nice.

JAN. Which is better?

MARLENE. Let me see the heel.

(**JAN** *lifts up her foot with the flat shoe.*)

MARLENE. Let me see the flat.

(**JAN** *switches feet.*)

They're both nice.

JAN. Leeny, listen. Are you going to get with the program or what?

MARLENE. What program?

JAN. What are we going to do with the house?

MARLENE. I just wish there was some way to keep it in the family.

JAN. Well, I'm sorry, but I think that's just selfish.

MARLENE. What about Beth's idea?

JAN. You're going to trust Beth to manage this place? Like she manages her personal life? Please.

MARLENE. What if I came up during the summers, too?

(**RON** *comes out of the bathroom and goes downstairs.*)

JAN. She doesn't want you here. She only wants the place for herself.

JAN. Look, what if one of your little students that you really liked finished second grade and they were all ready to go on to third grade, would you keep them in second grade just because you liked them so much?	**RON.** *(to* **ARTHUR***)* Where is everybody?
	ARTHUR. I don't know.
	RON. Oh, for–
MARLENE. No.	(**RON** *goes upstairs and knocks on the door to* **JAN***'s room. He looks inside and closes the door. He goes to the Green room.*)
JAN. You wouldn't keep them from going on to third grade, right? It wouldn't be right, right?	

MARLENE. Right.

JAN. Well, okay then. This little house has done everything it needs to do so now it's time for us to say goodbye and let it go.

(**RON** *enters.*)

RON. What's going on?

JAN. Ron, don't you think we should sell the house?

RON. I've always said this is the Levy house. The Levy girls should decide what to do with it.

JAN. Well, I don't know how you turn up your nose at two million dollars.

RON. Two million dollars? I thought it was a tear-down. You think you could get two million dollars for it?

JAN. I could get two million dollars for it.

RON. Two million dollars. Three way split?

JAN. After I take my commission.

RON. Of course.

JAN. *(referring to* **MARLENE.***)* Will you talk to her?

RON. Later, I'll talk to her. We have to go now.

(**JAN** *limps back to her room.*)

JAN. All right. All right. I'll be down in a minute.

(**RON** *turns to* **MARLENE.**)

RON. You told me she wanted to sell it. You didn't tell me you could get two million dollars for it.

MARLENE. It's not about the money.

RON. It is now. We'll talk about this later.

(**RON** *exits and goes downstairs.*)

(**BETH** *opens her door.*)

BETH. Sweetheart?

| **ARTHUR.** | **RON.** |
| Yes, dear. | Are you ready? |

BETH. *(to* **RON***)* I'm almost ready.

(to **ARTHUR***)*

Can you run out to the car and get me my hair brush, please? / It's in the glove compartment.

ARTHUR. Right.

RON. Your hair is fine.

BETH. Why don't you go ahead and we'll meet you there?

RON. We're all going in Joe's car.

BETH. *(cringing)* Oh, I don't want to go in Joe's car.

ARTHUR. What's wrong?

BETH. It has leather seats, doesn't it?

RON. I'm sure it does.

BETH. I can't ride in a car with leather seats.

ARTHUR.	**RON.**
Why not?	What? What are you, allergic to leather?

BETH. I can't stand the smell of leather. It makes me nauseated.

RON. I never heard of such a thing.

BETH. *(to ARTHUR)* Sweetheart, while you're in the car, pick out a couple of nice CDs so we have some nice music to listen to.

ARTHUR. Right.

BETH. And there are some plastic bags in the back seat. You'd better grab a couple, just in case.

RON. What do you need plastic bags for?

BETH. What if I vomit in their car?

RON. They'll buy a new one!

   (calling)

   Come on!

   (MARLENE gets up and exits the Green Room.)

BETH. *(to ARTHUR)* And make sure my water bottle is full, / would you, please?

RON. They have water in Three Oaks!

BETH. *(to ARTHUR)* And, Sweetheart, please try Dylan again, okay?

ARTHUR. I'll try.

BETH. Thank you.

   (ARTHUR goes out the front door. MARLENE comes downstairs.)

Oh, Leeny. Can I ask you a question?

MARLENE. Sure.

RON. We have to go-o!

BETH. I just need to ask her a question.

(**BETH** *takes* **MARLENE** *into the Gold Room and closes the door.*)

Why don't you come to the movie with us?

MARLENE. I'm doing laundry. I'll see you when you get back.

BETH. All right, listen. What did you think of my artists' colony idea?

MARLENE. I liked it.

BETH. So how do we convince the Queen?

MARLENE. I don't know.

BETH. If only we could buy her out of her share of the house.

MARLENE. That would take a lot of money.

BETH. The only one I know who's rich enough to buy her out is her. You'll back me up, right?

MARLENE. I have to go move the laundry.

(**MARLENE** *exits and heads for the basement.*)

RON. *(to* **MARLENE***)* Is she ready?

MARLENE. Almost. I thought I could ask people what they want for dinner.

RON. No, don't do that. / I'm trying to get out of here.

MARLENE. Then I could order and it'd be here / when you get back.

RON. Then it'll be cold. No, please. We've got to get going.

MARLENE. You're going to be hungry.

RON. We're not going to be hungry. We've got twenty-seven wagons full of popcorn.

(**MARLENE** *goes down to the basement as* **RON** *goes up to* **DYLAN***'s room. He knocks and enters.*)

RON. *(to* **DYLAN***)* Are you going to join the family and be a participant in your aunt's birthday celebration or are you going to continue to be a problem?

DYLAN. Those are my choices?

RON. Those are your choices.

DYLAN. Then I guess I'll go with problem.

RON. Just checking.

*(***RON** *closes the door and goes back downstairs.)*

*(***ARTHUR** *enters and goes to his bedroom and enters.)*

ARTHUR. *(to* **BETH***)* Here's your hairbrush.

BETH. Thank you.

*(***ARTHUR** *closes the door.)*

RON. Is she ready?

ARTHUR. Almost.

RON. Oh, for–

(He looks at his watch.)

We'll be lucky if we make it before the movie starts.

*(***ARTHUR** *goes to the kitchen and refills* **BETH***'s water bottle.)*

*(***YOUSEF** *enters.)*

RON. How're you doing?

YOUSEF. Very good.

RON. Can we go?

YOUSEF. I'm ready.

RON. Would you get your wife, please?

*(***YOUSEF** *goes upstairs.)*

Tell her to bring whatever face she's got on and let's go, all right?

*(***YOUSEF** *goes into his room.)*

YOUSEF. Can't we just go to dinner? Let's go to Timothy's.

JAN. We can't go to Timothy's. This is supposed to be our special family time. Isn't this special?

(sarconically) I can't believe I'm related to these people.

YOUSEF. They're crazy.

JAN. I talked to Marlene, but she just won't listen to reason.

(**ARTHUR** *is filling the water bottles.* **RON** *comes over to* **ARTHUR**.)

RON. I can't believe you've never seen *Mary Poppins*.

ARTHUR. My momma took care of other people's children. I didn't need to see a movie about it.

RON. If you were from Chicago, your momma might have been my momma's maid.

ARTHUR. You had a black maid?

RON. When I was growing up, yeah. Once a week.

ARTHUR. And I bet you called her the shvartza.

RON. Hey, that's not a derogatory term. Shvartza means black in Yiddish. It didn't mean - Hey. My parents were not prejudiced.

(calling out)

Let's go, people!

YOUSEF. *(to* JAN*)* What did you do when I told you I wanted to buy a Hummer?

JAN. I said, "Don't buy a Hummer."

YOUSEF. And what did I do?

JAN. You bought a Hummer.

YOUSEF. And then what did I do?

JAN. I don't know.

YOUSEF. I bought you that diamond necklace.

JAN. Ohmigosh! That's right. I forgot. You are the smartest man in the world.

(She gives him a kiss.)

YOUSEF. Let's go.

(**YOUSEF** *exits and goes downstairs.* **YOUSEF** *goes back to the kitchen and collects the popcorn.*)

(**ARTHUR** *knocks on* **DYLAN**'s *door and enters.*)

ARTHUR. *(cheerfully)* Hey, Champ, whad'ya say?

DYLAN. No!

ARTHUR. *(cheerfully)* Okay.

(**ARTHUR** *closes the door and goes back downstairs and goes into his room.*)

ARTHUR. Are we going?

BETH. Any luck with Dylan?

ARTHUR. It's going to be an ongoing process.

(**JAN** *comes downstairs and goes to the kitchen.*)

RON. Are you ready?

JAN. I'm ready.

(**RON** *goes to* **ARTHUR** *and* **BETH.**)

RON. Can we go, please?

BETH. I'm coming. I'm coming.

(**JAN** *brings bags of popcorn and hands them to* **RON.**)

JAN. Here, take these.

RON. All right. Let's go.

JAN. I just need to leave some food for Fifi.

RON. What?!

JAN. We're going to be gone for hours.

RON. All right. Forget it. I'm not going to the movie!

JAN. Will you–

RON. No! I'm not going! Forget it! The movie's going to be half over!

JAN. Go to the car. We'll be right there.

(**RON** *and* **ARTHUR** *exit out.* **BETH** *gathers up her purse.* **JAN** *goes to the kitchen.* **MARLENE** *comes up from the basement and goes upstairs to the Green Room.*)

JAN. *(to* **YOUSEF***)* Give me a Poochie Pizza.

YOUSEF. No, we're out of Poochie Pizzas.

JAN. We're out of Poochie Pizzas?

YOUSEF. She ate all the Poochie Pizzas.

JAN. I was sure...

YOUSEF. How about a Canine Cannoli?

JAN. This late in the day? She'll be up all night. Just give me a couple of cow's ears.

(**YOUSEF** *gets the box.*)

YOUSEF. Cherry, vanilla, or carob?

JAN. Give me the whole thing. Let her decide.

(**YOUSEF** *gives her the box of treats.*)

JAN. And bring her some water.

(**YOUSEF** *gets the water bowl and fills it.* **JAN** *takes the treats out the back.*)

(*offstage*) Hello, Fifi! Is that my good girl? Yes! That's my good girl! Does she want some treats?

(*Fifi barks offstage.*)

(**RON** *enters.*)

RON. Can we go, please?!!!

YOUSEF. We're going. We're going.

(**YOUSEF** *takes the water bowl outside.*)

RON. Where are you going?! Or for–

(**RON** *goes to* **BETH***'s room and enters.*)

RON. Oh, God, I miss you.

BETH. Ron.

RON. Meet me outside during the movie.

BETH. I can't.

RON. Once Mary, Bert, Jane, and Michael jump into the sidewalk drawing, there's eighteen minutes until they come back out.

BETH. Ron, please.

RON. Meet me in the parking lot.

BETH. I can't.

RON. You say you can't, but you don't say you won't.

BETH. I won't.

RON. Eighteen minutes. That's all I ask.

(*He exits.* **JAN** *and* **YOUSEF** *come in from the back.*)

RON. Now? Can we go?

JAN. All right. Let's go. I just want to say goodbye to Marlene.

RON. Come on!!!

(**JAN** *runs upstairs and goes into the Green Room.*)

JAN. (*to* **MARLENE**) I'll give you half my commission.

MARLENE. What?

JAN. When we sell the house. I'll give you half the commission. You could do a lot with that money.

MARLENE. It's not about the money.

JAN. Oh, Marlene. It's always about the money. Grow up.

(**JAN** *exits and goes downstairs.*)

(**ARTHUR** *enters.*)

RON. (*to* **ARTHUR**) Don't come in! Come on. We're going. Let's go.

(**ARTHUR** *exits.* **BETH** *enters. She starts to exit and then gets another idea.*)

BETH. Oh, wait. I just want to get a sweater.

RON. What for?!

BETH. I hate air conditioning. / It might be cold in the theatre.

JAN. Oh, that's a good idea.

(*to* **YOUSEF**)

Joe, get me a sweater. I can't run upstairs again.

YOUSEF. Which one?

JAN. Anything.

(**YOUSEF** *goes upstairs to his room.*)

RON. Come on!!!

(**ARTHUR** *comes in.*)

RON. (*to* **ARTHUR**) What?!

ARTHUR. I forgot my lyric sheets.

(**ARTHUR** *gets his lyric sheets and goes back out.* **YOUSEF** *comes downstairs with a sweatshirt for* **JAN.**)

YOUSEF. *(to* **JAN***)* How about this?

JAN. Not a sweatshirt.

RON. What's the difference?

JAN. *(to* **YOUSEF***)* Get me the yellow silk. In the bottom drawer.

*(***YOUSEF** *goes back upstairs to his room.)*

*(***BETH** *runs in and runs up to* **DYLAN***'s room.)*

BETH. I just want to try -

(She knocks on **DYLAN***'s door.)*

BETH. Honey?

DYLAN. No!

BETH. Okay.

*(***YOUSEF** *comes down with a sweater for* **JAN.** **BETH** *goes downstairs.)*

YOUSEF. Here.

JAN. Thank you.

BETH. Let's go.

RON. All right. Let's go.

*(***BETH** *exits.)*

JAN. All right. All right.

*(***JAN** *exits.* **YOUSEF** *exits.* **RON** *exits.)*

RON. Here we go.

*(***MARLENE** *comes up from the basement with a hamper full of laundry. The front door opens and* **JAN** *runs in and runs upstairs.* **RON** *follows.)*

RON. Now, what?!

JAN. I might need something to do during the movie. I just want to get my book of Sudoku.

*(***JAN** *runs into her room.)*

RON. AUGGGGHHHHH!!!!!!

(Fade out)

SCENE 2

(MARLENE is sitting on the couch, reading a book. She finishes the book and closes it.)

MARLENE. *(to the book)* Thank you.

(She puts the book down beside her, she looks around. She goes upstairs and knocks on DYLAN's door.)

Dylan?

DYLAN. What?!

(She cracks the door open)

MARLENE. It's me.

DYLAN. Oh, hey.

MARLENE. I was just wondering–

DYLAN. *(defensively)* I'm not doing anything.

MARLENE. I know, neither am I.

DYLAN. Oh.

MARLENE. I thought maybe we could do something together. How do you feel about Risk?

DYLAN. I try to avoid it.

MARLENE. No, I mean the board game, Risk. There's a whole box of board games downstairs. Would you like to play Risk?

DYLAN. I don't think so.

MARLENE. Boggle?

(No response)

Yahtzee?

(No response)

Scattergories?

DYLAN. No, thanks.

MARLENE. Okay. Well, it was just a thought. Your mom and everybody should be back soon. I think we're going to order in Chinese food. Is that good for you?

DYLAN. Yeah.

MARLENE. Okay. Well, I'll just...leave you alone.

(She closes the door and goes back downstairs. **DYLAN** *gets up, exits his room and goes halfway down the stairs.)*

DYLAN. Hey...I was going to tell you.

MARLENE. What?

DYLAN. When I was doing my thing...and you starting backing me up...that was cool.

MARLENE. Oh, well, I liked what you were doing. I guess I got kind of caught up in it. I hope you didn't mind.

DYLAN. No, it was cool.

*(***DYLAN*** comes downstairs and goes to the kitchen. He opens the refrigerator and gets something to drink.)*

MARLENE. Maybe we could go on the road together. "Two Live Jews."

(She expects a laugh from **DYLAN** *but doesn't get one.)*

MARLENE. Wasn't there a rap group called "Two Live Crew?"

DYLAN. Yeah.

MARLENE. So I was trying to do a thing on "Two Live Crew." "Two Live Jews." You know, sorry.

DYLAN. Your hip-hop references are a little out of date.

MARLENE. I'm sure they are.

(She points to his iPod.)

MARLENE. What are you listening to?

DYLAN. This is the new 50 Cent.

MARLENE. Can I hear it?

DYLAN. Sure.

(He gives her the earpiece, she puts it in her ear. He turns on the iPod. She listens for a bit. She then removes the earphones.)

MARLENE. Wow. Are you a big fan of Mr. Cent?

DYLAN. It's cool.

MARLENE. You know, you've always liked music.

DYLAN. I guess.

MARLENE. I remember at...one of your mom's weddings, you must have been seven or eight...

DYLAN. That was wedding number four. Larry the Lawyer.

MARLENE. Right, and everybody was kind of tense, I guess. Nobody was dancing. And I heard you say to your mother, "Everybody is like this."

(She goes ramrod straight.)

"Why isn't everybody like this?"

(She flops her arms and legs about.)

DYLAN. Did I do that?

MARLENE. Unfortunately, it didn't help much. Nobody thought Larry the Lawyer was going to last long.

DYLAN. He lasted four years. That puts him in second place.

MARLENE. Who was the longest?

DYLAN. The first one. Steve the Starter.

MARLENE. But you never knew him.

DYLAN. No.

MARLENE. Then came your dad.

DYLAN. Yeah, but they were only together for, like, a year.

MARLENE. But you see your dad.

DYLAN. In the summer usually.

MARLENE. How is that?

DYLAN. Okay, I guess. I get to go to California.

MARLENE. You get along with him okay?

DYLAN. We pretty much keep to ourselves. He got married again, you know.

MARLENE. No, I didn't.

DYLAN. Yeah, her name is Amber. She's six years, nine months and twenty-eight days older than I am.

MARLENE. No wonder he wants you to keep to yourself.

(moving on)

Who came after your dad?

DYLAN. There was Mike the Musician. I liked him. He would play the guitar and I would dance. But he took off. I never hear from him. And then there was Larry the Lawyer. I didn't like him much. He always beat me.

MARLENE. What?

DYLAN. Yeah. No matter what I tried, chess, checkers, ping pong, he always beat me at everything.

MARLENE. Wha...?

(It takes a moment for MARLENE to realize she's been set up.)

Oh!!

DYLAN. *(smiling)* Gotcha!

MARLENE. Wow. If you're going to have a sense of humor, I'm going to have to bring up my game.

DYLAN. You'd better.

MARLENE. Okay, then. So Larry the Lawyer "beat" you.

DYLAN. Yeah, but we never hear from him except for a Christmas card or something.

MARLENE. And that brings us to Arthur. How do you feel about Arthur?

DYLAN. He's okay, I guess. He's trying too hard.

MARLENE. At least he's trying.

DYLAN. I guess.

MARLENE. Do you know what a provost is?

DYLAN. No. He has meetings a lot. He knows a lot of people. He got me into my new school.

MARLENE. How is that?

DYLAN. Okay, I guess. We call it "Our Lady of Perpetual Medication."

MARLENE. What are you taking?

DYLAN. Right now, just Concerta for ADHD and Wellbutrin for depression.

MARLENE. Just?

DYLAN. They started me on Ritalin when I was eight. And Tofranil. And sometimes Risperdal. Then the Ritalin wasn't working I guess, so they switched me to Aderall. Then Aderall XR. And Lexapro. That was a wild combination. So they put me back on Ritalin. For a while, I'd take Ritalin in the morning, Dextrostat when I got home, and an Ambien at night to go to bed.

MARLENE. Wow.

DYLAN. It's all right. What gets me is when I want to go out and hang with friends, my mom says, "Have fun, Honey, but remember, don't do drugs."

MARLENE. She's concerned about you.

DYLAN. Yeah, I guess.

MARLENE. I was on Paxil for awhile.

DYLAN. How come?

MARLENE. A few years ago, Ron sent me to New York to a Social Anxiety Center. I called it the New York Home for the Chutzpah Challenged.

DYLAN. What did you do there?

MARLENE. Not much, really. I mean, can you imagine being in a roomful of extremely shy people? The highlight of the week was the Emily Dickinson Soundalike Contest.

DYLAN. So what happened?

MARLENE. They sent me home with a vat full of Paxil. It started to have an effect almost immediately. On the airplane home, I got everybody on the plane to sing, *My Kind of Town.*

DYLAN. Wow.

MARLENE. Yeah. It was…extraordinary. I was less shy. But I was less Marlene.

DYLAN. I hear that.

MARLENE. I stopped taking the Paxil. I think Ron's been kind of dissapointed.

DYLAN. You seem okay to me.

MARLENE. Well, thank you. You seem okay to me, too.

DYLAN. Thank you.

MARLENE. So, in general, how are you feeling?

DYLAN. Like I always feel.

MARLENE. How is that?

DYLAN. I don't know.

(Pause)

I have a lot of anger.

MARLENE. That's what I hear.

DYLAN. *(confessing)* But, sometimes, I don't know if I act like an angry kid because I'm angry or because everybody treats me like "The Angry Kid" so that's what I'm supposed to do.

MARLENE. Yeah, it's tricky, isn't it. I was always "The Shy Girl." Even times when I didn't want to be. But if people treat you like a particular thing long enough, it can be hard to convince them you're not just that thing.

DYLAN. Yeah, that's it, isn't it? I'm angry so people start treating me like that thing, that "Angry Kid," and that just makes me more angry.

MARLENE. Sure.

DYLAN. I don't want to be treated like a thing, I want to be treated like a person.

MARLENE. Of course you do.

DYLAN. Damn.

MARLENE. Really.

DYLAN. I'm going to get angry.

MARLENE. Okay, then I'm going to get shy.

DYLAN. *(stopping)* All right. All right. Let's not.

MARLENE. I'm lucky because I found Lily to help me when I don't want to be shy.

DYLAN. Lily is the...?

(He pantomimes the ventriloquist doll.)

MARLENE. Right. You've met.

DYLAN. You know, my mom thinks you're nuts.

MARLENE. What do you think?

DYLAN. I don't know.

MARLENE. Well, it's nice that you don't just take your mother's word for it.

DYLAN. Hey, my mother's been married five times. How sane is that?

(**MARLENE** *shrugs.*)

I'll tell you what, though. Aunt Jan and Uncle Yousef? I think they're nuts.

MARLENE. Everybody has their own mishegoss.

DYLAN. Their own what?

MARLENE. Mishegoss. It's like, your personal stuff. My mom, your grandma, used to say, "Crazy does not have a country. Everybody has their own mishegoss." Everybody has their own nutiness.

DYLAN. I guess. *(ruminating)* Life is weird, huh?

MARLENE. Oh, life is fine. Relatives are weird.

DYLAN. I guess.

(*Pause.*)

You're really good with that ventriloquism thing.

MARLENE. You think so? Thank you.

DYLAN. Do you think I could try it?

MARLENE. You want to try it? Sure. Don't go away.

(*She gets up and goes upstairs to her room to get* **LILY**. **DYLAN** *goes over and sits on the couch.* **MARLENE** *comes downstairs with* **LILY**.)

LILY. *(to* **DYLAN***)* Hello! I was hoping you'd call.

(*to* **MARLENE**)

He's hot.

MARLENE. I know.

DYLAN. Can I try?

MARLENE. Sure.

(*She takes* **LILY** *off her hand and hands her to* **DYLAN**.)

Just sit her in your lap. Now put your hand in back here.

(**DYLAN** *starts to put his hand into* **LILY**'s *back.*)

LILY. Watch it!

(**DYLAN** *takes his hand out*)

DYLAN. What?

MARLENE. It's okay, go ahead.

(**DYLAN** *inserts his hand.*)

LILY. Gently!

(**DYLAN** *freezes.*)

MARLENE. It's all right.

DYLAN. This is freaking me out.

MARLENE. It's okay. Put your hand all the way up there. That's it. Now, you see. You can move her mouth.

(**DYLAN** *does it*)

DYLAN. Now what?

MARLENE. Now, say, "Lily, I heard you went to see a therapist."

DYLAN. Lily, I heard you–

(to **MARLENE***)*

She's in therapy?

MARLENE. Oh, sure.

DYLAN. Lily, I heard you went to see a therapist.

MARLENE. Now, in Lily's voice say, "That's right. He said I'm a teepee and a wigwam."

DYLAN. *(in a high-pitched voice)* That's right. He said I'm a teepee and a wigwam.

MARLENE. But when she talks, move her mouth and it'll look like she's saying it.

(**DYLAN** *repeats while moving* **LILY**'s *mouth*)

DYLAN. *(in a high-pitched voice)* That's right. He said I'm a teepee and a wigwam.

MARLENE. Good. Then you say, "A teepee and a wigwam?"

DYLAN. A teepee and a wigwam?

MARLENE. And then Lily says, "Yeah. He said I'm two tents."
DYLAN. *(in a high pitched voice)* That's right–
MARLENE. Move her mouth.

(**DYLAN** *talks and moves* **LILY**'s *mouth*)

DYLAN. *(in a high-pitched voice)* Yeah. He said I'm two tents.
MARLENE. Now do the whole thing.
DYLAN. Lily, I heard you went to see a therapist.

(**LILY**)

That's right. He said I'm a teepee and a wigwam.

(**DYLAN**)

A teepee and a wigwam?

(**LILY**)

Yeah. He said I'm two tents.

MARLENE. There you go. That's your first ventriloquist's joke.
DYLAN. But my lips were moving.
MARLENE. So that just takes some practice.
DYLAN. That's pretty cool.
MARLENE. You could do this.
DYLAN. No, this is what I'm thinking. I don't like people who treat me like a thing instead of a person. But you treat a thing like a person instead of a thing.
MARLENE. I guess.

(**JAN** *enters.*)

JAN. *(to* **BETH***)* They're going to kill each other.

(**ARTHUR** *and* **RON** *enter followed by* **BETH** *followed by* **YOUSEF**)

ARTHUR.	**JAN.**
No, no. That's not the point.	*(from upstairs)* Would somebody please start pouring the wine? *(she goes into the bathroom.)*

RON.
> That is the point. It's a Disney movie.

ARTHUR.
> Exactly. That's the problem.

RON.
> You're the one with the problem.

ARTHUR.
> The anti-feminist message alone–

RON.
> What anti-feminist message?

ARTHUR.
> Are you kidding? The mother is a suffragette. She is singing about rights for women.

RON.
> It's a / great number.

BETH.
> *(to* **DYLAN***)* Hi, Honey.

DYLAN.
> Hi.

BETH.
> What are you doing?

DYLAN.
> Aunt Marlene is showing me how to do ventriloquism.

BETH.
> *(looking at* **MARLENE***)* Leeny. What are you doing?

MARLENE.
> We were talking.

BETH.
> You were talking.

DYLAN.
> Mom. It's all right.

ARTHUR.
And at the end, she takes her sash and blissfully uses it as a tail for the kite.

ARTHUR.
> There's an inherent anti-feminist message.

BETH.
> Well, I'm sorry. I don't think that's appropriate.
>
> *(to* **MARLENE***)*

RON.
> Then why does everybody there seem to be having such a good time?

ARTHUR.
> Because they've been mesmerized by the bombardment of lights and colors.

RON.
> So all the people there, all the millions and millions of people who have seen–

Would you put that thing away? Please?

(Marlene takes Lily and puts her aside.)

Honey, I'm sorry. I'm not feeling well. I have such a tummy ache. Would you go into my bathroom and bring me the Pepto Bismol, please?

(DYLAN does so.)

ARTHUR. I don't know what you're so enamored of. You were gone for almost twenty minutes.

RON. I was in the lobby. The popcorn machine broke down.

YOUSEF. *(to RON)* You see, I don't have that problem.

(MARLENE begins serving glasses of wine to RON and ARTHUR.)

RON.
> It doesn't matter, I've seen *Mary Poppins* many times.

BETH. *(to DYLAN, as he brings Pepto Bismol)* Thank you, Honey.

ARTHUR. I wouldn't brag about it.

RON. Well, excuse me, Mr. Intellectual. Maybe next time we can see something more worthy of your superior intelligence. How about "Sing Along *Citizen Kane?*"

BETH. Ron, come on.

RON. He started it.

BETH. I started it.

(**MARLENE** *hands a glass of wine to* **BETH**.)

(*to* **MARLENE**) Can I drink wine with Pepto Bismol?

MARLENE. Why not?

BETH. Anyway, all I said was Walt Disney's *Mary Poppins* is a lot different than P.L. Travers' *Mary Poppins*.

ARTHUR. And therein lays the tragedy.

RON. (*to* **MARLENE**) You hear that? *Mary Poppins* is a tragedy.

(**JAN** *comes downstairs.*)

JAN. You know what's the problem with *Mary Poppins*? All the nannies have seen it. They come in with, "I'll stay until the wind changes." There's no commitment. There's no loyalty. You know who makes the best nannies really? Gay men. We call them "Mannies."

(*to* **YOUSEF**) Remember Jack? He was great with the kids. He was the best.

YOUSEF. He was gay?

ARTHUR. I don't understand why anyone would want to see this movie today.

RON. You don't understand–

ARTHUR. It's the Disneyized version of the perfect family. Mother will stay home and take care of the children. Father will be hard working but in touch with his feelings. Mary Poppins can just fly away.

BETH. If Mary Poppins flew away today she'd be burned up in the ozone layer.

JAN. Mary Poppins would never get hired today.

| **BETH.** | **ARTHUR.** |
| That's true. | I think you're right. |

JAN. Would you entrust your children to Mary Poppins?

| **JAN.** | **ARTHUR.** |
| No way. | I think not. |

JAN. She takes the children out of the house without telling anyone where she's going. She puts them in hazardous situations. Up on the rooftop.

ARTHUR. Into the sidewalk.

BETH. She gives the children medicine without a prescription.

ARTHUR. She convinces them to give their money away.

JAN. She's a socialist!

BETH. And then she abandons the children. She just takes off.

ARTHUR. That's going to mean a lot of therapy.

BETH. And what about Bert?

JAN.	**ARTHUR.**
Bert!	Bert, who lives in the street!

JAN. The children are hanging out with homeless people!

BETH. He should be on the neighborhood registered sex offender list.

JAN.	**ARTHUR.**
Yes!	Definitely.

RON. All right! All right! Can I just say…right now Walt Disney is spinning in his grave.

BETH. Really? I thought he was frozen.

RON. No.

JAN. Yeah. I thought he was in a block of ice / underneath the Pirates of the Caribbean.

ARTHUR. Cryogenics.

RON. No, that's an urban myth.

ARTHUR. Really.

RON. Yes.

ARTHUR. Because I always thought that would be poetic justice for Walt Disney. After making all those cartoons, to be in suspended animation.

BETH. Very good.

JAN. That's a good one.

BETH. *(to* **ARTHUR***)* I'm sorry you had to have a debate about *Mary Poppins*.

ARTHUR. No, no. That's quite all right. I don't mind an intellectual thrust and parry. The Transcendentalists - Emerson, Bronson Alcott, Margaret Fuller - would often come together to discuss philosophy...poetry... the essence of religion.

JAN. Can we order now? I'm starving.

YOUSEF.	**RON.**
Yes.	All right. / Let's eat.

BETH. Me, too.

JAN. Who's got the thing?

(**MARLENE** *hands the takeout menu to* **JAN.**)

JAN. Okay, what does everybody want? I want Moo Goo Gai Pan.

RON. Pepper steak.

(*to* **MARLENE**)

Marlene? Pepper Steak.

MARLENE. That's fine.

RON. Can we get some egg rolls?

JAN. How many egg rolls?

(**RON** *and* **MARLENE** *raise their hands*)

RON.	**BETH.**
Two for us.	(*to* **DYLAN**) Honey, do you want an eggroll?
JAN.	**DYLAN.**
Two for you. One for me.	K.
(*to* **BETH**)	**BETH.**
	(*to* **ARTHUR**) Sweetheart?
Beth?	**ARTHUR.**
	Yes, please. I'll have one.

BETH. Yes, one each.

JAN. Three orders of egg rolls.

BETH. Dylan likes chicken fried rice.

JAN. We can get some chicken fried rice.

BETH. *(to* **ARTHUR***)* Sweetheart, do you want to order an entree and then we'll all share?

ARTHUR. Sure. Put me down for sweet and sour shrimp.

JAN. Sweet and sour shrimp.

RON. *(interrupting)* Uh...no.

ARTHUR.	**BETH.**
No?	What?

JAN. What's the problem?

RON. We don't eat shrimp.

BETH.	**JAN.**
What?!	What are you talking about, we don't eat shrimp?

BETH. We eat shrimp.

RON. We don't eat shrimp.

BETH. Ron, we eat shrimp.

RON. Not in this house.

BETH.	**JAN.**
What?!	What are you talking about?

RON. In the fifteen years since I've been a part of this family, we have never eaten sweet and sour shrimp.

BETH.	**JAN.**
I'm sure we have.	I just don't like it. I don't like the sauce. It's too sweet.
RON.	**YOUSEF.**
No, we haven't.	I'll eat it.

RON. *(to* **YOUSEF***)* I'm sure you would.

   (to **BETH***)*

   I was once in this very kitchen with your mother and I suggested a shrimp dish and she said, "I don't eat shrimp."

JAN. She didn't like it.

BETH. I think she was allergic.

RON. She didn't eat shrimp because this is a Jewish house.

JAN. Since when is this a Jewish house?

RON. That was your mother's way of life / and I think we should respect that.

BETH. Ron, if you want to express your anger / there are more appropriate ways.

RON. I'm not angry. This has nothing to do with anger.

JAN. Ron, let the man order what he wants.

RON. No.

JAN. You don't have to eat it.

RON. No.

JAN. Joe doesn't drink but it doesn't bother him if–

RON. This isn't his house.

JAN. This is his house as much as it's your house.

RON. Not if I'm the only one who cares about protecting the Jewishness of this house.

JAN. This isn't a Jewish house!

RON. Not to you. You gave up being Jewish / when you married an Arab.

JAN. I didn't give up being Jewish.

YOUSEF. *(to* **RON***)* I'm not Arab. I'm Persian.

RON. Oh, right. Persian. I'll call you when I need a rug.

BETH.	**JAN.**
Ron, stop!	All right, that's enough.

YOUSEF. No, no, no. That's all right. I get it.

> *(to* **ARTHUR***)* Hey, Arthur. *(quoting)* Two Jews walk into a bar. A week later, they own it.

RON. That's very funny.

> *(***RON** *notices that* **ARTHUR** *is laughing.)*

RON. What are you laughing at?

ARTHUR. That is such a well-constructed joke. In just two lines, he encapsulates everything that Shakespeare lays down in *The Merchant of Venice*.

RON. Oh, great! Now we're all Shylocks!

ARTHUR. People, people, please. I'm the newest member of the family. I certainly don't want to be the cause of an inter-family imbroglio.

RON. "Imbroglio?"

ARTHUR. *(to* **JAN***)* I believe I misspoke before. I don't want sweet and sour shrimp.

JAN. You're sure?

ARTHUR. Yes.

JAN. You can if you want.

ARTHUR. No, really. I don't want sweet and sour shrimp.

JAN. All right. What would you like?

ARTHUR. Sweet and sour pork.

BETH. Sweetheart.

JAN. Yes!

RON. What exactly is your problem?

ARTHUR. I don't have a problem. I don't have a problem. I want to know what's your problem?

JAN. Let's have sweet and sour pork.

RON. You want to know what my problem is?

RON. No.

JAN. There's pork in the eggrolls.

ARTHUR. Yes, I want to know. Tell me what your problem is. Go ahead.

RON. No, there isn't.

RON. You want to know what my problem is? You're my problem.

JAN. There's pork in the eggrolls, goddamit!

ARTHUR. I'm your problem. Isn't that a surprise.

RON. Then don't order eggrolls!

RON.
    Yes! You're my problem.

ARTHUR.
    Man, you have been on me since I walked in the door.

RON.
    Hey she picked you. I didn't.

JAN.
    I'm ordering eggrolls! Lots and lots of eggrolls! Pork eggrolls! Shrimp eggrolls!
    (to **YOUSEF***)*
    Give me the goddamn phone.

ARTHUR. And that bothers you, doesn't it?

RON. I'm just wondering how you got to be flavor of the month.

BETH. *(pleading)* Ron, please.

ARTHUR. *(to* **RON***)* And it really irks you that the flavor of the month is chocolate.

RON. "Irks" me? No, that's not / what "irks" me.

ARTHUR. What you'd really like is for me to be the shvartza around here, isn't it?

RON. No.

ARTHUR. Your problem is that you have a problem with black people.

RON. That is not true. And even if it was, so what? You with your "irks's" and "imbroglios." The fact is, you're not very black are you?

ARTHUR. I'm black enough to kick your ass!

BETH.
    No, please.

JAN.
    All right, guys. / Come on.

RON. You want a piece of me?

ARTHUR. I want a sizable piece of you.

RON. You want to step outside?

ARTHUR. Let's step outside.

    (**RON** *heads for the door*)

RON. Let's go.

ARTHUR. Let's go

JAN. Guys.

BETH. Please don't do this.

(**RON** *gets to the door and opens it*)

RON. After you.

(**ARTHUR** *exits.* **RON** *closes the door and walks away from it.*)

Do you believe this guy?

(**ARTHUR** *comes in through the door.*)

ARTHUR. I have never in all my existence–

(**RON** *turns and starts to hop around like he's in a boxing ring.* **ARTHUR** *just stands and stares at him.*)

RON. Come on...Take your best shot.

(**BETH** *steps up to intervene.*)

BETH.	**RON.**
Ron...Ron, please... *(sings)* JUST A SPOONFUL OF SUGAR HELPS THE MEDICINE GO DOWN THE MEDICINE GO DOWN MEDICINE GO DOWN.	Come on...What are you going to do? Hit me with a rhetorical remark?...Come on...Slay me with a well chosen metaphor? *(But then he gets a side stitch and has to stop.)*

ARTHUR. *(to BETH)* I think I should go.

BETH. No. Arthur–

ARTHUR. I'm not comfortable here.

BETH. I'm sorry.

ARTHUR. No. I'm sorry. I think I've made a mistake.

BETH. No. Please, Sweetheart. Come on. You said you'd never leave me.

ARTHUR. And you said you come from a nice, normal family.

(to the others) For the record, I think most of you are insane.

BETH. *(to ARTHUR)* I'm sorry.

ARTHUR. Maybe I can catch a train to Chicago.

BETH. No. Please.

JAN. It's not a bad idea, Beth. Why don't you both go?

BETH. *(snapping)* I don't need your advice, thank you.

JAN. I'm just suggesting –

BETH. I know what you're suggesting. You want us to leave, don't you?

(to basically everyone, referring to ARTHUR) The way you have treated this man has been inexcusable. I bring my husband to meet my family.

(to JAN) Was that your plan from the beginning? Do everything you can to make him as unwelcome as possible?

JAN. *(sarcastically)* Yeah, sure. That was the plan.

BETH. Maybe my marriage doesn't mean anything to you–

JAN. Well, maybe your marriage doesn't mean anything to you. How should I know?

BETH. The choices I have made -

BETH.	**JAN.**
In my life are my choices and I take responsibility for them and if you ever respected me instead of judging me like you're the queen of the world–	Well, you bring the husband in...We get to know him...And then he disappears... You're like Penn and Teller.

(ARTHUR takes BETH's hand.)

ARTHUR. Beth. Beth. Come with me. We'll both go.

BETH. No.

(referring to JAN) You can't trust her. We go out that door, we turn around, and she'll have sold the place out from under us.

JAN. What do you think I'm going to do? Sell the house to the first person that walks by?

BETH. You are not selling this house.

JAN. And how are you going to stop me? Move in with an army of starving artists?

BETH. If that's what it takes to keep you from stealing it from us.

JAN. Don't start with stealing, Beth. I swear to God.

BETH. What do you call it? You take whatever you want–

JAN. So do you.

BETH. Whenever you want–

JAN. So do you.

BETH. So that makes you a thief.

JAN. You're the thief! You're the thief! You stole Marty Klein!

BETH. I did not steal Marty Klein. He preferred me to you. What could I do?

JAN. You could've stayed home instead of following us to Touhy Avenue Beach and waving your tush in front of his face.

BETH. I did not wave my...Oh, for god sakes, you want Marty Klein so much, you can have him. I'll give you his number, you can call him.

JAN. *(aghast)* You have Marty Klein's phone number?

BETH. He called me. Last year. He got divorced. He just called me to check in. We're old friends.

JAN. We're old friends. He didn't call me.

BETH. You're married.

JAN. That never stopped you.

BETH. Don't go there.

JAN. Don't make me go there.

BETH. *(to* **ARTHUR***)* All right. Let's get out of here.

(to **JAN***)* We will be back. Soon. If you so much as take a single item out of any of those boxes, I will sue you, I swear.

JAN. Because you know where to get a lawyer, don't you?

BETH. *(to* **ARTHUR***)* All right. Let's go.

JAN. I am sick and tired –

JAN.	**BETH.**
Of being the bad guy around here. You pass yourself off as Little Miss Innocent. Marian the Librarian. *(referring to* **ARTHUR***)* Does he know about you?	No. I am sick and tired of you thinking that just because you have money, that gives you the right to be in charge of everybody and everything.

JAN. *(cont.)* Does he know about the astronomical number of men you've been with?

BETH. The number of men I have been with is none of your business.

*(***MARLENE** *has put* **LILY** *on and comes forward with her.)*

LILY. Quiet!

JAN. Marty Klein was my business! Marty Klein / was my business!

BETH. Forget about Marty Klein!

LILY. Quiet!!

JAN. *(to* **BETH***)* You stole Marty Klein from me!

LILY. Quiet!!!

JAN. You stole Marlene's husband from her!

(Now, it's quiet.)

YOUSEF. Okay. I think we'll go to Timothy's now.

(He goes to **JAN** *and leads her out.)*

Good night all.

*(***YOUSEF** *and* **JAN** *exit.)*

BETH. Arthur.

*(***ARTHUR** *puts up his hand to keep her away. He turns and exits.)*

Oh, no. Please, no.

(She exits out after him.)

RON. Marlene.

LILY. Well, what do we have here?

RON. Please don't do that.

LILY. The children have been misbehaving, Ms. Levy.

*(**RON** exits out the back. **DYLAN** comes up to **MARLENE** and **LILY**.)*

DYLAN. I'm sorry.

LILY. I feel very sad.

DYLAN. Me, too.

LILY. *(to **MARLENE**)* What are we hanging around here for?

MARLENE. I don't know, Lily. I don't know.

DYLAN. I was thinking I could really go for a game of Risk right now. Or Boggle? Or Yahtzee?

(fade out)

SCENE 3

(At rise: **JAN** *is in her room, packing.* **ARTHUR** *is in his room, packing.* **DYLAN** *is in his room, packing.* **RON** *is in his room, passed out on the bed.* **BETH** *is in the living room combing through a box of papers.)*

(Fifi barks offstage.)

*(***MARLENE** *enters through the back door.* **BETH** *looks up and sees her.)*

BETH. Oh, my God. Where have you been?

MARLENE. I've been walking.

BETH. All night? I've been worried sick.

MARLENE. I slept for awhile on the beach. But mostly, I've been walking. I thought I should get used to being homeless.

BETH. Leeny, you're not homeless.

MARLENE. Well, I don't think I can be here anymore. And I don't want to go to my house in Chicago, so...I am without a home.

BETH. Oh, Leeny. I'm so sorry. Please believe me. I was weak. I was stupid. I don't know what I was thinking. I wasn't thinking. I was alone. I was lonely. I know that doesn't excuse it. I need... You know what I need. Hell, I'm on my fifth marriage.

MARLENE. Are you and Arthur okay?

BETH. Yes. Yes, thank God. Actually, we had the best talk. He's such a mensch. I don't deserve him.

MARLENE. No, you probably don't.

(She cringes.)

Uh. I'm sorry. I don't want to be sarcastic.

*(***JAN** *has come out of her bedroom and downstairs.)*

JAN. Well...This is a suprise. I didn't expect to see you two talking to each other.

BETH. You're the one I'm not talking to.

JAN. Well, that's convenient. Because I'm not speaking to you either.

(to MARLENE) Joe went out. As soon as he gets back, we'll be leaving.

MARLENE. What?

BETH. And Arthur and I will be leaving shortly.

MARLENE. No. No. Guys. Come on. We can figure this out.

JAN. I don't think it's likely that any agreements will be reached by further discussion at this time.

BETH. That's all you have to say to Marlene?

JAN. Maybe we can all get together and work things out some other time…In forty or fifty years.

BETH. Oh, come on. I don't expect you to apologize to me.

(referring to MARLENE) But don't you think you owe her an apology?

JAN. Apology? For what? For telling the truth?

(acquiescing) All right. All right.

(pronouncing) I'm sorry…If my speaking the truth caused anyone any undue discomfort.

BETH. *(incredulous)* Oh, my god.

MARLENE. Jan. Isn't there some way we can work things out?

JAN. We couldn't even make it through a week together.

MARLENE. We used to be close.

JAN. We were never that close.

MARLENE. Sure, don't you remember? The three of us, holding hands, playing on the beach? At night, we'd play games or go bowling? Or Dad would take us to Bergers so we could get a corned beef sandwich and a chocolate phosphate? Remember that big guy behind the counter and he had that big pencil and he'd write the prices right on the brown paper bag?

(Pause.)

JAN. I have no memory of any of that.

(reflectively) I know I came down here for something.

(remembering) Oh...

(**JAN** *goes over to the boxes, reaches in, and removes the stamp collection.*)

I'm taking this.

BETH. Jan.

JAN. I'll get the best price I can for it and add it to the estate.

BETH. Jan. Leave it.

JAN. I'm taking it.

MARLENE. Please, please, please! Stop! My God, we have got to come to some understanding. We have to find some common ground. Can we just, for a start, agree to disagree?

(**JAN** *and* **BETH** *look at each other and then back at* **MARLENE.**)

BETH. No.

JAN. No. I don't think so.

(**MARLENE** *turns and goes upstairs.*)

JAN. *(to* **BETH***)* As soon as Joe gets back, we'll be leaving.

(She turns to go upstairs.)

BETH. Jan.

(**JAN** *stops and turns back.*)

JAN. What?

BETH. Did you ever hear of anyone named Giuseppe Orson Doyle?

JAN. No. I haven't read every book ever written like you have.

(**JAN** *goes up to her room.*)

(**MARLENE** *enters her room.* **RON** *stirs and wakes up.*)

RON. Ohmigod. Are you all right? I've been looking everywhere for you.

MARLENE. I'm all right.

RON. I was about to call the police.

MARLENE. I'm all right.

RON. I heard people were packing up. Withdrawing from the field of battle, as it were.

MARLENE. Yes.

RON. I figured we might as well take off, too.

MARLENE. Sounds like a plan.

RON. All right. We need to talk.

MARLENE. I don't have anything to say.

RON. And that's what we have to talk about. You could holler. You could call me names. You could hit me.

MARLENE. Would that make you feel better?

RON. I want you to do what would make you feel better.

MARLENE. I do have one question.

RON. Ask me anything.

MARLENE. Exactly how many times did you sleep with my sister?

RON. Only once. Last summer.

(beat)

And one time, the summer before that.

(beat)

And one time, the summer before that. That's all, I swear. It was right after she got dumped by Larry the Lawyer. She needed comfort.

MARLENE. And what did you need?

RON. Look, my career's going nowhere. We know that. You and I haven't exactly been...We know that. Anyway, we were all together up here and...it happened.

MARLENE. Have there been others?

RON. Other women? No. I swear. I could handle a "same time, next year" thing, but...No. No. I really just wouldn't have the energy.

(beat)

RON. Do you have any other questions?

MARLENE. Not at this time.

RON. Then the defense rests. I'll start packing up the car.

(**RON** *takes a couple of suitcases downstairs and out.*)

(**ARTHUR** *enters with suitcases.*)

ARTHUR. *(to* **BETH***)* I'm all set to go when you are.

(**JAN** *comes downstairs with a suitcase.*)

(to **JAN***)* Are you taking off?

JAN. Pretty soon.

ARTHUR. Well, it's certainly been quite an experience getting to know the Levy family.

JAN. Yeah. Let me know when the Post Traumatic Stress kicks in.

ARTHUR. Are you just going to close up the house?

JAN. My friend at the real estate office will keep an eye on it.

BETH. But she's not going to put it on the market.

(**YOUSEF** *enters.*)

YOUSEF. She doesn't have to put it on the market. I'm going to buy it.

BETH. But we're not going to sell it.

YOUSEF. Oh, yes, you will. I'll pay two point five million. You'll take it.

JAN. Why would you–

YOUSEF. We have over an acre of land. We have a hundred feet of road frontage. My architect says we can put up six to eight units.

JAN. No. You'd never get zoning for it. Not in Union Pier.

YOUSEF. Yes, you will.

JAN. No. This is a high erosion area. The local zoning people would never allow it.

YOUSEF. Yes, they will. I made friends with people on the committee. Next week, the man from Environmental Quality is coming to do the inspection.

JAN. When were you planning on telling me?

YOUSEF. I wanted it to be a surprise.

(beat)

For your birthday.

(beat)

Happy Birthday.

(beat)

Total market value - Five to six million dollars.

JAN. *(dumbfounded)* Five to six million?

ARTHUR. And that becomes part of the estate?

YOUSEF. Ehhhhh...No. But you still get your share of the purchase price.

(with great magnanimity) And for anyone in this family who wants to buy, I give you ten per cent off pre-construction price.

BETH. Except for one thing.

YOUSEF. What?

BETH. Giuseppe Orson Doyle.

YOUSEF. What is that?

BETH. Giuseppe Orson Doyle.

JAN. So who is he?

BETH. You said the taxes on the house are paid by the estate account?

JAN. Yeah.

*(**BETH** holds up a piece of paper.)*

BETH. Well, here's last year's tax bill. And it's addressed to Giuseppe Orson Doyle.

JAN. Let me see that.

(She takes the bill and peruses it.)

JAN. It's this address. Who the hell is Giuseppe Orson Doyle?

BETH. I have no idea.

(**DYLAN** *enters, carrying his duffel bag.*)

BETH. Honey, you ever hear Papa mention anyone named Giuseppe Orson Doyle?

DYLAN. No.

JAN. *(calling out)* Marlene!

(**MARLENE** *comes downstairs with* **LILY**'s *case.*)

MARLENE. What?

JAN. You ever hear of anyone named Giuseppe Orson Doyle?

MARLENE. No.

(**RON** *enters.*)

JAN. Ron, you ever hear of anyone named Giuseppe Orson Doyle?

RON. Oh, sure.

JAN. You have?

RON. Back in the 60s, he was a small time hood in the Chicago Mafia.

JAN. Mafia?

RON. Yeah, Giuseppe Orson Doyle. They called him "the Mop" because he was part Mick and part Wop.

YOUSEF. How do you know this?

RON. My dad served on an organized crime commission. They investigated all those guys. Sam Giancana, Tony Accardo, Rocco Fischetti. I don't know what happened to Doyle. Why do you ask?

BETH. Well, evidently, he owns this house.

RON. *(jawdropping)* What?!

JAN. His name is on the tax bill.

RON. Let me see that.

(**JAN** *hands him the tax bill.*)

YOUSEF. We have to do a title search.

(**YOUSEF** *takes out his cell phone.*)

Wait one minute.

(He dials.)

(into phone) Barbara? Hello. How are you?...You have the address of where I am?...I want you to call Chicago Title. Ask for Rick. Tell him to do a Title Search for this property. Tell him it's for me. Do it now. I'll hold on.

(to the others) Take two minutes.

(Everyone stands and waits.)

BETH. Would Dad have given him the house without telling us?

JAN. If Dad gave him the house, there should be a Quit Claim Deed.

BETH. I looked. It's not here.

RON. Maybe the house was always Doyle's. They say a lot of the old Mafia guys had houses up here.

JAN. So what are you saying? Our father was buddies with old Mafia guys?

BETH. So maybe he did have a secret life. "Leonard Levy, Dentist to the Mob."

(**YOUSEF** *hears something on his phone.*)

YOUSEF. *(into phone)* Yes?...Go ahead...Giuseppe Orson Doyle. Got it. Thank you. Goodbye.

(He hangs up.)

JAN. *(to* **BETH** *and* **MARLENE***)* We don't own this house.

(**BETH** *gets an idea.*)

BETH. Wait a minute.

(**BETH** *reaches into one of the boxes and finds what she is looking for. She holds up the photo of Dad and the other guy.*)

BETH. Remember this picture of Dad and this other guy? I wonder...

(She slips the back of the frame off and looks at the back of the picture.)

Yes.

(reads)

"To Dr. Levy. Thanks for straightening out my teeth. And my life. G.D."

(displaying the picture.)

Ladies and Gentlemen, meet Giuseppe Orson Doyle.

JAN. We need to get in touch with Mr. Doyle.

YOUSEF. I bet he has no idea what the market value of the property is.

JAN. I'll lowball him and you come in with a better offer. We'll still come out ahead.

RON. Yeah, yeah, yeah. First, you have to find him. If he's still alive. He could be anywhere. In a Witness Protection Program. Or at the bottom of Lake Michigan.

*(**BETH** gets another idea.)*

BETH. *(gasping)* Huh!

(She reaches into a box and brings out the shoe.)

BETH. What if this is his shoe? This could be evidence in a murder.

*(to **RON**)*

Did he have both legs?

RON. I couldn't say.

*(**BETH** gets another idea.)*

BETH. Wait a minute. Wait a minute. There were some letters. Where did I put them?

(She goes to a box and removes the stack of letters. She takes the top one and opens it.)

BETH. *(reading)* "July 15, 1965."

(She turns the letter over.)

Signed "G.D."

(She turns the letter back over.)

(reading)

"Dear Lenny. They thought if they killed my wife they could shut me up. And they were right. I'm gone. I can't tell you where I'm going because it's not safe for you to know. But I do want you to know that you and the missus were the nicest people I ever met. I hope I'll see you again sometime. Here are the keys to the lake house. I know you and the missus enjoyed it. Use it whenever you want. And I know this is a lot to ask, but please, please, please. Take care of my baby. She's a good girl. She's quiet. You'll hardly know she's there. I'll come back next summer if I can. Or the summer after that. Arriverderci, Doc. G.D."

*(Eventually, everyone looks at **MARLENE**. Eventually, **MARLENE** stands up.)*

MARLENE. I'm the daughter of a gangster?

(Pause.)

BETH. That's why you're so tall!

MARLENE. *(to* **JAN** *and* **BETH***)* Did you know?

BETH. No.

JAN. No. I swear to God.

MARLENE. Why wouldn't they tell me?

BETH. They wanted you to feel safe.

JAN. They were probably scared to death.

MARLENE. They wanted to protect me. So no one could do to me what they did to my...mother.

*(**JAN** goes to **MARLENE**.)*

JAN. Hello, I'm Jan Levy with Caldwell Banker. You have a lovely home here. I'm familiar with the market and I'm sure I could get you a good price for it.

(RON *steps in.*)

RON. *(to* MARLENE*)* I'll handle this.

(to JAN*)* I understand you have a client who's interested in the property. Write up an offer and we'll take it under consideration.

MARLENE. Ron.

RON. Yeah.

MARLENE. Get the hell out of my house.

RON. But...

MARLENE. Take the car. Drive away.

(RON *turns and exits.*)

MARLENE. *(to* JAN*)* I'm not interested in selling at this time.

JAN. Well, then. I'll guess we'll be going now.

(to YOUSEF*)* Take this to the car. I'll go get Fifi.

MARLENE. Jan.

(MARLENE *goes to* JAN *and embraces her.*)

I still think you're my sister.

(JAN *returns the embrace and then looks at* MARLENE.)

JAN. I suppose this means you should have the stamps, too.

(JAN *hands the book to* MARLENE.)

MARLENE. Thank you.

(JAN *exits out the back.* MARLENE *goes to* YOUSEF *and gives him a hug.*)

MARLENE. Goodbye, Joe.

YOUSEF. Arriverderci.

(YOUSEF *goes out the front.*)

ARTHUR. *(to* MARLENE*)* Can we give you a ride back to the city?

MARLENE. You go. I'm staying here.

ARTHUR. But–

MARLENE. This is my home. Maybe this is the summer he'll come back.

BETH. Leeny?

(**BETH** and **MARLENE** embrace.)

BETH. Will you be okay?

MARLENE. Yes.

BETH. How does The Doyle Center for the Arts sound to you?

MARLENE. I'll think about it.

(referring to the boxes)

And I'll go through all of that. I'll make a complete inventory and send you an itemized list.

(**BETH** turns to **DYLAN**.)

BETH. Honey, we're going now.

DYLAN. Mom.

BETH. What, Honey?

(**DYLAN** turns to **MARLENE**.)

DYLAN. Could I hang out here?

BETH. What?

DYLAN. Just for the summer.

MARLENE. Okay.

BETH. Your father's expecting you.

DYLAN. I'll talk to him.

BETH. But, you can't stay here. You–

ARTHUR. Beth.

(to **DYLAN**) Is this really what you want to do?

DYLAN. Yes. I will live my life deliberately.

BETH. But what will you do? How will you manage?

DYLAN. (to **MARLENE**) Well, what do you think? You cook. I'll wash. And Lily dries.

MARLENE. Sounds good to me.

BETH. But–

ARTHUR. Beth. Let's go.

(to **DYLAN** and **MARLENE**) Good luck.

(DYLAN and MARLENE wave. ARTHUR escorts BETH out. MARLENE and DYLAN look at each other. MARLENE puts on some music. MARLENE brings out LILY. MARLENE, LILY, and DYLAN dance.)

(Fade out)

END OF PLAY

Set design by Jom C. Stark

OTHER TITLES AVAILABLE FROM SAMUEL FRENCH

AFFLUENZA!

James Sherman

Comedy / 4m, 2f / Interior

A hilarious new play from James Sherman, *AFFLUENZA!* borrows classic characters from Restoration Comedy like the cuckolded husband, the coquette, the wily servant, and the fop to create a contemporary comedy of manners. When multi-millionaire, William Moore brings home his new girlfriend, his son and ex-wife are threatened by the potential new heir to the family fortune. Who gets what and who ends up with whom is revealed in this dazzling display of wit and wordplay.

"James Sherman has created a Moliere play for our times. A clever and delightful piece of theatre."
– *Chicago Reader*

"James Sherman's *Affluenza!* is an impressive piece of work – a witty balancing act that gets laughs from age-old human foibles as well as our present age of untrammeled corporate greed."
– *The Kansas City Star*

"Sherman's vital Americanese displays all of the lightness, gaiety and poetic skill of the French satirist's classic French."
– *The Atlanta-Journal Constitution*

SAMUELFRENCH.COM

OTHER TITLES AVAILABLE FROM SAMUEL FRENCH

BEAU JEST

James Sherman

Comedy / 4m, 2f / Interior

Sarah is a nice Jewish girl with a problem: her parents want her married to a nice Jewish boy. They have never met her boyfriend, a WASP executive named Chris Kringle. She tells them she is dating a Jewish doctor and they insist on meeting him. She plans a dinner party and, over the heated protests of Chris, employs an escort service to send her a Jewish date to be Dr. Steinberg. Instead, they send Bob Schroeder, an aspiring actor who agrees to perform the impersonation. Happily, he is extremely convincing in the role and Sarah's parents are enraptured. Soon, even Sarah falls for Bob.

"A light, sweet romantic comedy."
– *Chicago Tribune*

"Hilarious and quite moving. Sherman wonderfully blends farce with a genuine insight."
– *Chicago Sun Times*

"Very funny…The well crafted play has a lot to say about nuclear families of any ethnic persuasion."
– *Wall Street Journal*

SAMUELFRENCH.COM

OTHER TITLES AVAILABLE FROM SAMUEL FRENCH

MAGIC TIME

James Sherman

Comedy / 5m, 3f / Interior set

Off Broadway audiences and critics enjoyed this engaging backstage comedy about a troupe of actors preparing to give their last summer performance of *Hamlet*. Cleverly, the backstage relationships mirror the onstage ones. Larry Laertes resents David Hamlet since he feels he should have that role. Also, he is secretly in love with Laurie Ophelia, who is living with David and trying to get him to be honest with her about his feelings. There's a Horatio who has a career in TV commercials, a Polonius who gave up acting to have a family and teach but has second thoughts, and a Gertrude and Claudius who are married.

"There is an artful innocence....It is also delightful."
– *The New York Times*

"Captivating....It is entirely winning."
– *The New York Daily News*

SAMUELFRENCH.COM

www.ingramcontent.com/pod-product-compliance
Lightning Source LLC
Chambersburg PA
CBHW070645300426
44111CB00013B/2263